Czechoslovakia and Yugoslavia: The History and Legacy of the Multiethnic Nations that Split Apart after the Cold War

By Charles River Editors

The flag of Yugoslavia

About Charles River Editors

Charles River Editors is a boutique digital publishing company, specializing in bringing history back to life with educational and engaging books on a wide range of topics. Keep up to date with our new and free offerings with this 5 second sign up on our weekly mailing list, and visit Our Kindle Author Page to see other recently published Kindle titles.

We make these books for you and always want to know our readers' opinions, so we encourage you to leave reviews and look forward to publishing new and exciting titles each week.

Introduction

Czechoslovakia's coat of arms

"No country of people's democracy has so many nationalities as this country has. Only in Czechoslovakia do there exist two kindred nationalities, while in some of the other countries there are only minorities. Consequently in these countries of people's democracy there has been no need to settle such serious problems as we have had to settle here. With them the road to socialism is less complicated than is the case here. With them the basic factor is the class issue, with us it is both the nationalities and the class issue. The reason why we were able to settle the nationalities question so thoroughly is to be found in the fact that it had begun to be settled in a revolutionary way in the course of the Liberation War, in which all the nationalities in the country participated, in which every national group made its contribution to the general effort of liberation from the occupier according to its capabilities. Neither the Macedonians nor any other national group which until then had been oppressed obtained their national liberation by decree. They fought for their national liberation with rifle in hand. The role of the Communist Party lay in the first place in the fact that it led that struggle, which was a guarantee that after the war the national question would be settled decisively in the way the communists had conceived long before the war and during the war. The role of the Communist Party in this respect today, in the phase of building socialism, lies in making the positive national factors a stimulus to, not a brake on, the development of socialism in our country. The role of the Communist Party today lies in the necessity for keeping a sharp lookout to see that national chauvinism does not appear and develop among any of the nationalities. The Communist Party must always endeavour, and does endeavour, to ensure that all the negative phenomena of nationalism disappear and that people are educated in the spirit of internationalism." - Tito

On New Year's Day 1993, Czechoslovakia broke into two separate countries, the Czech Republic and Slovakia. Thus ended one of the creations brought about by the Treaty of Versailles after World War I, and as a country that had existed for just under 75 years, Czechoslovakia spent most of its time under the tyranny of fascism or communism.

Of course, the country's origins go back far longer than the 1910s, and they were complex and convoluted. The very geography of central Europe meant this territory had been conquered and occupied many times over the course of history, and for much of the modern era, the area belonged to much larger empires, including the Holy Roman Empire, the Austrian Habsburg Empire, and finally the Austro-Hungarian Empire. Nevertheless, two distinct ethnicities had come to make up the bulk of the territory's inhabitants: the Czechs, predominantly in the areas of Bohemia and Moravia, and the Slovaks, in Slovakia. Both peoples had their own Slavic-based languages, but the languages were similar enough to be mutually intelligible.

Despite any ethnic similarities, the country that formed in 1918 among the ashes of the Austro-Hungarian Empire was by no means a "nation-state" as most people understand that term. In fact, much of the territory which bordered Germany was inhabited by ethnic German speakers, including one of Prague's most famous sons, the writer Franz Kafka. One of the 20th century's most celebrated authors spoke German as his first language. As such, the lands that became Czechoslovakia had usually existed in some kind of supranational system where identity was allowed to be relatively fluid.

Czechoslovakia would also play a crucial role in bringing about World War II, a sign that the area's nationalism, which ultimately split Czechoslovakia apart in 1993, had long spelled danger in a place where so many groups competed for power. The presence of German speakers would serve as a pretext for Hitler's acquisition of the Sudetenland, creating a crisis ahead of history's deadliest war and serving as a harbinger of things to come.

Czechoslovakia's split was mostly peaceful, which stands in stark contrast to that of Yugoslavia, arguably one of the most unusual geopolitical creations of the 20th century. The Yugoslav state had never existed in any historical sense, and the ties that bound together its constituent peoples were tenuous at best. Although nominally all "Slavs," the country was an amalgamation of languages, alphabets, cultures, religions and traditions, which ensured its short existence was littered with splits, conflicts, and shocking violence. In a sense, it's somewhat surprising that it lasted as long as it did.

In the wake of World War I, as the political boundaries of Europe and the Middle East were redrawn, the Kingdom of Yugoslavia, initially known as the Kingdom of Serbs, Croats and Slovenes, came into existence with a monarch as its head of state. Confirmed at the 1919 Versailles Conference, the "first" Yugoslavia was a particularly fragile enterprise, and there was almost constant tension between the majority Serbs and the other Yugoslav nationalities, especially the Croats. As a result, the Kingdom was a land of political assassinations, underground terrorist organizations, and ethnic animosities. In 1929, King Alexander I suspended democracy and ruled as a dictator until he himself was assassinated in 1934.

The Kingdom of Yugoslavia was particularly vulnerable to the forces that engulfed the rest of Europe at the end of the 1930s, including fascism and communism. When the Axis forces attacked in 1941, the country quickly capitulated and was dismembered by the Nazis and their allies. A separate Croatian state was formed, led by Ante Pavelić, who committed some of the worst crimes and human rights abuses of the war. The Balkan region was virtually emptied of its Jewish population, victims of the Nazi Holocaust.

From the beginning, fascism was opposed by two major groups in the region, the monarchist Chetniks and the communist Partisans. The latter, led by Josip Broz Tito and backed by the democratic powers, emerged in the dominant position at the end of the war. The World War II era produced many leaders of titanic determination, men whose strengths and weaknesses left an extraordinary imprint on historical affairs, and the struggle between massively divergent ideologies catapulted some individuals unexpectedly onto the world stage. Marshal Tito was undoubtedly one of these figures. Originally a machinist, Tito leveraged his success in the Communist Party of Yugoslavia (CPY) and a number of extraordinary strokes of luck into dictatorial rule over Yugoslavia for a span of 35 years. World War II proved the watershed that enabled him to secure control of the country, leading an ever more powerful army of communist partisans against both the Germans and other Yugoslav factions. During the war, SS leader Heinrich Himmler himself begrudgingly stated, "He has really earned his title of Marshal. When we catch him we shall kill him at once...but I wish we had a dozen Titos in Germany, men who were leaders and had such resolution and good nerves, that, even though they were forever encircled, they would never give in.

During his reign, Tito managed to quash the intense national feelings of the diverse groups making up the Yugoslavian population, and he did so through several methods. He managed to successfully play the two superpower rivals, the United States and Soviet Union, off against each other during the Cold War, and in doing so, he maintained a considerable amount of independence from both, even as he additionally received foreign aid to keep his regime afloat. All the while he remained defiant, once penning a legendary letter to Joseph Stalin warning the Soviet dictator, "To Joseph Stalin: Stop sending people to kill me! We've already captured five of them, one of them with a bomb and another with a rifle... If you don't stop sending killers, I'll send a very fast working one to Moscow and I certainly won't have to send another."

Never afraid to use political murder when expedient, yet simultaneously outgoing and good-humored to those around him, Tito created a unique and unusual state between the Western democracies and the Eastern Bloc. Only upon his death did the fabric of the state tear asunder and age-old identities reassert themselves, bringing about a period of intense conflicts that produced a new equilibrium with ethnically-based successor states that cracked up the state he once led. Cold War rivalries also provided Yugoslavia with a geopolitical significance that evaporated after the fall of the Berlin Wall. Without its charismatic dictator who transcended national rivalries and two superpowers interested in its stability, Yugoslavia collapsed within the space of a few short, bloody years in the 1990s.

Internal issues plagued the country in its final years and Tito had tinkered with Yugoslavia's constitution on several occasions. His final attempt, in 1974, saw the partial separation of Kosovo – crucial in the Serb national story – from the rest of Serbia. A number of reasons led to the rising Serb nationalist sentiment after Tito's death, but Kosovo was a central aspect. Yugoslavia required far-sighted, magnanimous leaders to avoid internecine disputes, but none were available, or at least in positions of power in the 1980s. In Croatia, Franjo Tudjman – a long time Croat nationalist – emerged as the republic's leader, and Slobodan Milošević rose to prominence in the middle of the decade and, despite apparently being a career communist, positioned himself as "defender of the Serbs." He began ousting his rivals and installing sympathetic underlings into leadership positions in Kosovo, Vojvodina, and Montenegro, essentially giving him a majority bloc at the federal level.

Depending on the source, many authors have focused on different catalysts for Yugoslavia's demise, but Vesna Drapac may have succinctly summed the situation up when he wrote that by the end, the state "lacked a reason to exist." There is certainly something in this sentiment, but the disintegration came at an enormous cost.

Czechoslovakia and Yugoslavia: The History and Legacy of the Multiethnic Nations that Split Apart after the Cold War examines how the multicultural nations were founded, the inherent tensions there, and how everything fell apart. Along with pictures of important people and places, you will learn about Czechoslovakia and Yugoslavia like never before.

Czechoslovakia and Yugoslavia: The History and Legacy of the Multiethnic Nations that Split Apart after the Cold War

Czechs and Slovaks before 1918

Before the formation of Czechoslovakia near the end of 1918, both Czechs and Slovaks lived within the Austro-Hungarian Empire. The Habsburg dual monarchy system meant that rulers in Vienna and Austria controlled the western portion of the empire, while rulers in Hungary and Budapest were in charge of the eastern side. Altogether, the Habsburgs ruled over a huge multiethnic swathe of territory, and it was said that at the start of the First World War in 1914, Vienna was the most vibrant international city in the world. Broadly speaking, the Czechs were located under Austria's more liberal rule while the Slovaks were under the control of the more authoritarian Hungarians.

The Habsburgs may have overseen a relatively benign empire, but pressure from national groups like the Czechs and Slovaks were building in the late 19th century. Prague, the Czech capital, was one of Europe's grandest cities, full of baroque architecture and impressive demonstrations of power. As the Kingdom of Bohemia, the region had thrived under both Holy Roman and Austrian Habsburg's loose confederation of states, kingdoms, and principalities. Bratislava, Slovakia's capital, was smaller than Prague but nevertheless charming and historic.

The tension in the area was symptomatic of what was occurring in Europe as a whole. At the end of the 19th century, there existed in Europe an interconnected series of alliances, treaties and pacts, both overt and secret, that were intended to maintain the balance of power and the status quo on the mainland, the likes of which had never been seen before. The purpose of this web of alliances was ostensibly to ensure peace, but in reality it meant that an aggressive power could wage small-scale wars with virtual impunity thanks to the looming threat of a full-scale escalation on the European mainland, as had occurred during the Schleiswig-Holstein Question and the Franco-Prussian War (both conflicts started by what was now Germany).

The first of these alliances emerged in the wake of the Napoleonic Wars with the creation of the Holy Alliance, a "triumvirate" of Austria, Russia and Prussia. 60 years later, Otto von Bismarck, perhaps the greatest politician of his age (and certainly the most effective champion of the Prussian cause), created the *dreikaiserbund*, the League of the Three Caesars, a re-affirmation of the previous alliance renegotiated to include Germany. Fittingly, this alliance fell apart over the Balkans, as Russia and Austria-Hungary were at odds over how to administer and exert influence across the region. Thus, in 1879, Germany and Austria-Hungary dropped Russia as a partner to form the Dual Alliance, and three years later, Austria set aside its differences with Italy, which had recently fought two viciously contested wars of independence against Austria to achieve sovereignty. Together, these three nations formed the Triple Alliance.

Bismarck

Things held together (albeit in an extremely fragile fashion) until roughly 1890, shortly after the ascension to the throne of Germany of Kaiser Wilhelm II. Wilhelm was concerned about the vast and shadowy power still wielded by Bismarck, so he compelled Bismarck to resign out of fear that he would undermine the legitimacy and power of the German monarchy by being the de facto ruler. This was a legitimate fear given that the diplomatic circles of Europe still contacted Bismarck over matters of international policy thanks to their decades-long familiarity with him. What Wilhelm failed to take into account was just how much Bismarck had wielded his personality, ruthlessness, personal magnetism and sheer diplomatic brilliance to keep Germany safe and ensure its constant expansion despite the minefield of European politics. With Bismarck gone, the fragile, informal diplomatic ties he had maintained disintegrated, and in 1890 the Kaiser committed a serious political blunder by refusing to renew the Re-Insurance Treaty, which guaranteed mutual non-aggression between Russia and Germany. Russia then went on to sign the Franco-Russian Alliance with France in 1902, effectively hemming in Germany between two largely hostile powers. France also signed a treaty with Britain, the Entente Cordiale, and in 1907 Britain involved itself further in European affairs by signing the Anglo-Russian Convention. These were not formal alliances, but for simplicity's sake, this complex Anglo-Russian-French arrangement is usually referred to as the Triple Entente. While there were no formal guarantees that Britain would intervene if either France or Russia were attacked or went to war, they certainly strengthened the possibility that this would occur.

Matters in Europe were further complicated by the massive escalation of an arms race. In the wake of the Franco-Prussian War of 1871, Germany had established itself as the dominant power in Europe, and German industrial output had grown by orders of magnitude. By the dawn of the 20th century, Germany was even competing with the mighty Royal Navy for domain over the world's oceans, an impressive output for a country that had never truly made naval power a priority. The *Kaiserliche Marine*, with its modern destroyers, worried the British so much that in 1906 they launched HMS *Dreadnought*, the most powerful battleship of its time. This race for technological supremacy was as much saber-rattling as it was a genuine policy to ensure sufficiently modern equipment in fear of an attack by another European great power, but regardless, military spending almost doubled among most of the powerful nations. Moreover, virtually all nations adopted new breech-loading bolt-action rifles to go along with new artillery pieces, heavy and super-heavy mortars and railway guns, machine guns, grenades, poison gas shells, and a host of other instruments of destruction. As a result, weapons were becoming deadlier and more powerful just as nations like Germany and Italy were following burgeoning imperialistic agendas, and just as the British and French sought to prevent their expansion.

Meanwhile, Bohemia exerted pressure on Vienna at the end of the 19th century, demanding greater autonomy and eventually drawing concessions from the Austrians, who promised the Czechs reforms. These were never to materialize, however, as Vienna stalled on its promises while drifting through geopolitical crises in the first decade of the 20th century.

The Balkans have historically been one of the world's most combustible regions. Home to several national groups and at a crossroads of Europe, Asia and the Middle East, the Balkans have exerted an outsized role on world affairs. Infamously, the assassination of Austrian Archduke Franz Ferdinand by a Serb nationalist, Gavrilo Princip, caused the dominoes to fall, leading to the First World War.

The Balkans, however, had been flammable long before Princip's bullets murdered the Austrian monarch-in-waiting. A number of countries had attempted to expand their borders within the Balkan region, and many of these had been supported by larger continental powers, such as Russia, Britain, France, Austria, Germany, and Italy. The main cause of this instability was the decline of empire in the Balkans. The Ottoman Empire had held sway over the southeast section of the Balkans since the 15th century, while the Austrian Habsburgs were dominant in the northwest of the region, but both empires moved into relative decline in the 19th century, albeit in different ways. The Ottoman territories were slowly lost to other encroaching forces, while the Austrians (and then Austro-Hungarians) actually expanded until the First World War. This turned out to be a case of "imperial overstretch," and as the two hegemons weakened, a number of political spaces opened up.

The Slovaks too, were unhappy with their position within the empire and had to endure "Magyarization," or encroaching Hungarian influence, during this period. While the Czechs organized, however, many Slovaks emigrated, particularly to the United States. The best-known personification of the former trend was the rise of Tomáš Masaryk in the late 19th century and early 20th century. Masaryk became the great figurehead for an independent Czechoslovakia, but in his early political days he styled himself as a reformer, not a separatist. The most vocal opponents of the Czech autonomy campaigns were ethnic Germans living in Bohemia, commonly known as "Sudeten Germans," who were animated by a greater sense of German identity after 1871 and resented Czechs who were asserting their own, potentially exclusive status.

The Balkans' Different Ethnic Identities

"If you humble yourself too much, you will get trampled on." – Ancient Serbian proverb

Though the Turkish persecution of the Serbians under the Ottoman Empire is a part of Serbian history that is often swept under the rug, their descendants never forgot the seemingly endless trials of their ancestors. The Muslim Turkish rulers not only set out to erase the Serbian social elite, they were determined to sever the Orthodox Christian roots its population desperately clung to. Those who could afford it fled to neighboring nations for refuge, while the rest were ejected from their rightful lands, left with no choice but to set up camp in "hostile mountains."

The homes and properties of all Orthodox Christian Serbians were promptly confiscated by Turkish authorities, and the bulk of the people were unwillingly tethered to a system of serfdom under their foreign masters, otherwise known as the "*giours.*" Their new subjects, the Serbian masses, were derogatorily referred to as the "*rayah,*" meaning "the herd." Even worse were the suffocating laws that singled out the Christian Serbs. They were only to possess mules, leaving horses, camels, and other "superior" means of travel for Turkish and Muslim use. On that note, they were never to ride a mule in the presence of a Muslim, nor could they own houses or other property that would outshine a Turkish abode. Fantastic churches and *rayah* buildings were torn down in droves, and what was left of them in pitiful conditions at best, their church bells rusting over from neglect. Needless to say, erecting new ones was out of the question. The *Rayah* were forbidden from burying their dead in broad daylight, nor could they utter the name of Christ in the presence of a Muslim.

Turkish sultans kidnapped generations of Christian Serbian children – some say up to 5 million – to equip their slave-fueled Janissary armies under a system called the *"devsirme."* Authorities whipped these boys into shape, and exploiting their Stockholm syndromes, implanted in their young minds a ride-or-die loyalty for their captors. Many Ottomans abused their privileged positions, the worst of them employing the *jus primae noctis*, or the "right of the first night." Plainly put, Turkish men were granted first dibs on Serbian servant women on their wedding nights, a humiliating practice that carried on until the 19th century. The list of injustices seemed to stretch on for miles.

There existed a door that guaranteed one access to a much brighter future, but like most entries, it came attached with a price of admission. A Serbian had to formally renounce their Christian faiths and embrace the Ottoman brand of Islam. Only then would the rights of a "full citizen" be bestowed upon them. Many struggled at the crossroads. Some, fretting over the futures of their loved ones, made the tentative step over the line, whereas most refused to budge, digging their heels into the ground.

The early 1800s brought about the first wave of Serbian insurgencies. The Serbians rejoiced as the revolutionary leader, a ferocious man known only as Karađorđe ("Black George"), took matters into his own hands and beheaded the quartet of Janissaries previously heading Serbia, relieving the people from the crush of their heels. By December 1806, Karađorđe and his troops had seized Belgrade, soon to become its capital.

Karađorđe

For the next 7 years, the Serbians ran their own ship, giving them their first, albeit fleeting, taste of freedom. Karađorđe was named the Grand Vožd of Serbia, and in 1808, a constitution of Serbia's own was published. Not only did Christian churches appear again, a string of Serbian schools were established in Belgrade, one of which eventually blossomed into a prestigious university.

By October 1813, however, Turkish soldiers swarmed into Serbia once more, replanting their flags in Belgrade in short order. As the story goes, Turkish authorities, infuriated by the Serbians' insubordination, allowed their soldiers to slay any Serbian over the age of 15 and enslave as many maidens and children as they could get their hands on for a period of two weeks. Up to 1,800 Serbian slaves were sold in a day.

Rather than submit to the Ottomans, the Serbian hunger for independence only grew more powerful. While much of their physical culture had been destroyed by their oppressors, subsisting only on a few epic poems about Serbian victories on the battlefield and the like, the Serbian spirit had not lost its character. The Serbian community not only held strong to their Orthodox Christian beliefs and distinctive cultural traits, their increasing exposure to foreign democracies continued to fan the flames of their patriotism.

Merchants who journeyed to Habsburg-operated Hungary with stacks of plump, acorn-fed pork in their wagons were some of the first to dip their toes into the light at the end of the tunnel. This was a place that treated Christians – albeit German Catholics – with due respect, and it appeared to accept the Orthodox Serbian neighbors with little to no hesitation. A few Serbians even held posts in Hungarian administrative offices and enlisted for the Austrian side during the Austro-Turkish War. It was here that they picked up on Hungarian military tactics and organizational skills that allowed them to secure their seven year spell of independence. They also found a father figure of sorts in Russia, for this modern "Slavic and Orthodox country" had become a formidable threat to the Ottomans.

More Serbians began to chase trade and educational opportunities beyond the border, and as such, they explored unfamiliar, but groundbreaking schools of thought in regards to philosophy, law, politics, and societal values shaped by rationalist and romanticist ideals. Serbian scholars left and right attempted to revitalize the local culture. Dositej Obradovic, a traveling monk, not only translated a number of foreign texts, he spun together a series of dictionaries and grammatical textbooks penned in the modern Serbian tongue. Another Enlightenment-era wordsmith, Vuk Karadzic, churned out collections of epic poetry dedicated to Serbian identity, many of its values sympathizing with the peasant communities.

By 1867, the Principality of Serbia would be awarded some semblance of independence, but the 1878 Congress of Berlin cemented the Austrian administration's position behind the scenes. Many, particularly the peasant and newly-enlightened masses, saw this not only as a stall in progress – to subject themselves to outside authority would mean taking a tremendous step backwards. It would not be long before their suspicions were realized, for Serbian conservatives, many of them supposedly puppets of the Austrians, began to drive a rift between the local patrician and plebeian classes. Only Serbian elites were inducted to civil office and awarded privileges the peasant classes were robbed of, for the plebeians were deemed too uneducated and incompetent to handle governmental affairs. What was more, the voices of the peasantry were often silenced; those who spoke out against the government were immediately tossed behind bars on the charge of public disobedience.

Belgrade pulsed with the cries of liberal university students who sided with the plebeians, many lambasting the conservatives for their "draconian legislation and hollow...corrupt system of administration." The discontent among the masses continued to swell, spawning an epidemic of overzealous, fanatical nationalism. This phenomenon was anything but lost on one notorious underground syndicate known as the "Black Hand," which would capitalize on these feelings of frustration and resentment to push for the creation of a Greater Serbia. So potent was their vision that they were willing to go to any extreme to secure it.

In order to fully understand the implications and motivation for the Black Hand's actions, it's necessary to understand the situation in Serbia and the Balkans as a whole, and why a small region whose chief importance in the previous centuries had been as a battleground for the great powers to control access to Europe became responsible for the outbreak of World War I. Three years after Archduke Franz Ferdinand's birth, in 1878, the Great Powers signed the Treaty of Berlin, a document intended to pacify the Balkans, where the Ottoman Empire had been forced to use brutal force to suppress rebellion on more than one recent occasion. Among other clauses, the Treaty empowered the Austro-Hungarian Empire to take nominal charge of the Bosnia District of the Ottoman Empire, although it officially remained Turkish territory. At the same time, the Treaty also acknowledged the sovereignty of the Principality (later the Kingdom) of Serbia, under the aegis of King Milan Obrenovic, whose family was closely connected to Emperor Franz Joseph's and was well-liked at court. This diplomatic connection helped ensure stability within a notoriously volatile region; administrative power passing to a European power with a Christian government and a long-term vested interest in the East helped quell much of the turmoil to which the Balkans had been subject to under Ottoman rule, while Serbia provided a useful and friendly bulwark to calm any unrest which might occur.

The tension in the Balkans was symptomatic of what was occurring in Europe as a whole. In the briefest of terms, by 1900 there existed in Europe an interconnected series of alliances, treaties and pacts, both overt and secret, that were intended to maintain the balance of power and the status quo on the mainland, the likes of which had never been seen before. The purpose of this web of alliances was ostensibly to ensure peace, but in reality it meant that an aggressive power could wage small-scale wars with virtual impunity thanks to the looming threat of a full-scale escalation on the European mainland, as had occurred during the Schleiswig-Holstein Question and the Franco-Prussian War (both conflicts started by what was now Germany).

The first of these alliances emerged in the wake of the Napoleonic Wars with the creation of the Holy Alliance, a "triumvirate" of Austria, Russia and Prussia. 60 years later, Otto von Bismarck, perhaps the greatest politician of his age (and certainly the most effective champion of the Prussian cause), created the *dreikaiserbund*, the League of the Three Caesars, a re-affirmation of the previous alliance renegotiated to include Germany. Fittingly, this alliance fell apart over the Balkans, as Russia and Austria-Hungary were at odds over how to administer and exert influence across the region. Thus, in 1879, Germany and Austria-Hungary dropped Russia as a partner to form the Dual Alliance, and three years later, Austria set aside its differences with Italy, which had recently fought two viciously contested wars of independence against Austria to achieve sovereignty. Together, these three nations formed the Triple Alliance.

Bismarck

Things held together (albeit in an extremely fragile fashion) until roughly 1890, shortly after the ascension to the throne of Germany of Kaiser Wilhelm II. Wilhelm was concerned about the vast and shadowy power still wielded by Bismarck, so he compelled Bismarck to resign out of fear that he would undermine the legitimacy and power of the German monarchy by being the de facto ruler. This was a legitimate fear given that the diplomatic circles of Europe still contacted Bismarck over matters of international policy thanks to their decades-long familiarity with him. What Wilhelm failed to take into account was just how much Bismarck had wielded his personality, ruthlessness, personal magnetism and sheer diplomatic brilliance to keep Germany safe and ensure its constant expansion despite the minefield of European politics. With Bismarck gone, the fragile, informal diplomatic ties he had maintained disintegrated, and in 1890 the Kaiser committed a serious political blunder by refusing to renew the Re-Insurance Treaty, which guaranteed mutual non-aggression between Russia and Germany. Russia then went on to sign the Franco-Russian Alliance with France in 1902, effectively hemming in Germany between two largely hostile powers. France also signed a treaty with Britain, the Entente Cordiale, and in 1907 Britain involved itself further in European affairs by signing the Anglo-Russian Convention. These were not formal alliances, but for simplicity's sake, this complex Anglo-Russian-French arrangement is usually referred to as the Triple Entente. While there were no formal guarantees that Britain would intervene if either France or Russia were attacked or went to war, they certainly strengthened the possibility that this would occur.

Matters in Europe were further complicated by the massive escalation of an arms race. In the wake of the Franco-Prussian War of 1871, Germany had established itself as the dominant power in Europe, and German industrial output had grown by orders of magnitude. By the dawn of the 20th century, Germany was even competing with the mighty Royal Navy for domain over the world's oceans, an impressive output for a country that had never truly made naval power a priority. The *Kaiserliche Marine*, with its modern destroyers, worried the British so much that in 1906 they launched HMS *Dreadnought*, the most powerful battleship of its time. This race for technological supremacy was as much saber-rattling as it was a genuine policy to ensure sufficiently modern equipment in fear of an attack by another European great power, but regardless, military spending almost doubled among most of the powerful nations. Moreover, virtually all nations adopted new breech-loading bolt-action rifles to go along with new artillery pieces, heavy and super-heavy mortars and railway guns, machine guns, grenades, poison gas shells, and a host of other instruments of destruction. As a result, weapons were becoming deadlier and more powerful just as nations like Germany and Italy were following burgeoning imperialistic agendas, and just as the British and French sought to prevent their expansion.

Nevertheless, the creation of Yugoslavia long predates the Cold War. It was a creature of the post-World War One settlement and of the Versailles Conference.[1] The country consistently lacked popular legitimacy, including during its first phase. The various component nationalities were suspicious of one another, particularly the smaller nations towards the majority Serbs. It is worth considering how the state of Yugoslavia came about at all. The answer lies in the particular confluence of geopolitics – the collapse of two huge empires, Austro-Hungary and the Ottomans – as well as a small but committed group of proponents. Crucially, during the First World War between 1914 and 1918, the Allied Great Powers - Britain, France and the United States – all quiesced to the foundation of Yugoslavia, or the Kingdom of Serbs, Croats and Slovenes.

Turmoil Before World War I

The Balkan area has historically been one of the world's most combustible regions. Home to several national groups and at a crossroads of Europe, Asia and the Middle East, the Balkans have exerted an outsized role on world affairs. Infamously, the assassination of Austrian

---

[1] Dejan Djokić, *Pašić & Trumbić: The Kingdom of Serbs, Croats and Slovenes.* (Haus Publishing, 2010)

Archduke Franz Ferdinand by a Serb nationalist, Gavrilo Princip, caused the dominoes to fall, leading to the First World War.

The Balkans, however, had been flammable long before Princip's bullets murdered the Austrian monarch-in-waiting. A number of countries had attempted to expand their borders within the Balkan region, and many of these had been supported by larger continental powers, such as Russia, Britain, France, Austria, Germany, and Italy. The main cause of this instability was the decline of empire in the Balkans; the Ottoman Empire had held sway over the southeast section of the Balkans since the 15th century, while the Austrian Habsburgs were dominant in the northwest of the region. Both empires moved into relative decline in the 19th century, albeit in different ways. The Ottoman territories were slowly lost to other encroaching forces, while the Austrians (and then Austro-Hungarians) actually expanded until the First World War. This turned out to be a case of "imperial overstretch," and as the two hegemons weakened, a number of political spaces opened up. The wake of World War I would produce a nation made up of Serbs, Croats, Bosnians, Slovenes, Macedonians, and Montenegrins. These nationalities, however, would not prove satisfactory for many in the new country, and others would later emerge, most notably the Kosovan Albanians and Bosniaks.

In addition to the nationalities that would be part of Yugoslavia, the Balkans was home to a number of other identities, ethnicities, and traditions, and the Greeks, Bulgarians, Romanians, Albanians and Turks would all play a role in the development of Yugoslavia as well.

As mentioned earlier, the Serbs had shown themselves to be potent adversaries in the Balkan region and prized themselves as warriors. Notions of a Serb-nation focused on the 1389 "Battle of Kosovo," on the "Field of Blackbirds," where the Ottomans had defeated a Serb army but nevertheless gave Serbia a sense of identity in a hostile region. Kosovo also became an integral part of any notion of a Serb state. As a predominantly Christian Orthodox people, Serbia also gained fraternal support from co-religionists, most notably Russia.

Croatia was the second largest of the Yugoslav nations. Croats were Catholic and saw themselves as more inherently part of European "civilization" compared to the other Yugoslav nationalities, though it should be noted that this sentiment was shared by most of the Slavic ethnicities. The region that incorporates modern Croatia was part of the Austrian Habsburg Empire for several centuries and gained some autonomy in 1868. Croatian nationalism had grown during the century, and a number of groups were agitating for full independence during the First World War.

Bosnia, meanwhile, was a more complicated area. Home to large minorities of self-described ethnic Serbs and Croats, the majority of Bosnians were Muslim, sometimes (later) known as Bosnian Muslims or Bosniaks. Bosnians had lived in the territory for centuries but enjoyed some preferential treatment under the Islamic Ottoman Empire. Nevertheless, a specific version of Bosnian nationalism grew during the 19th century, and the country – known as Bosnia and

Herzegovina – was occupied by Austria-Hungary from 1878 and annexed in 1908.

Slovenia, wedged between Austria, Italy, and Croatia at the foot of the Alps, was another Catholic area, but with its own unique language. Most of the other nationalities spoke a version of Serbo-Croat, even if the alphabets they used varied. Slovenia was part of the Austro-Hungarian Empire, but it also experienced a surge in nationalist sentiment, particularly after the continent-wide revolutions of 1848.[2]

Macedonians lived in the region bordering today's Greece, which was still part of the Ottoman Empire in the early 19th century, and Macedonia also bordered Albania and Bulgaria. Macedonia had particular links with the latter, including linguistically and culturally, and the territory included a significant minority of ethnic Albanians. Macedonia proved to have one of the most potent national movements of the era, manifesting itself notoriously as the Macedonian Revolutionary Organization (MRO), which, although relatively small in number, played a role in weakening the Ottoman Empire.

Montenegrins were the last piece of the ethnic jigsaw puzzle. Set on the Adriatic Sea, Montenegro had come under the control of the Ottomans, Habsburgs, and Venetians at various times. The tiny country gained principality status in 1852 and then full independence from the Ottomans in 1878. Traditionally, Montenegro had been close to Serbia and fought on the same side during the First World War, but it was occupied by Austrian forces between 1916-1918.

As the Austro-Hungarian and Ottoman Empires teetered in the late 19th century, Balkan countries all sought to expand their borders.[3] In their own ways, each Balkan nation had what was known as a "Big Idea" (from the Greek "Megali Idea"), a project to maximize its boundaries to the furthest possible point and incorporate various historical claims. The list of conflicts is long and perplexing, and it included the war between the Russians and the Ottomans that culminated in the 1878 Congress of Berlin, presided over by German Chancellor Otto von Bismarck. The year 1878 saw an increase in Serbia's territory, independence for other countries from the Ottomans, and the Austrian occupation of Bosnia and Herzegovina. The Treaty of San Stefano confirmed the territorial changes, in particular the enlargement of Bulgaria.

From the Congress of Berlin until 1914, Balkan countries would be locked into competition, making the region a cauldron of violence and instability.[4] In addition, the Great Powers felt compelled to involve themselves in the region. It appeared that Russia backed change and the dismemberment of the Ottoman Empire, whereas Britain seemed to support the status quo encapsulated by the existing situation.[5]

---

[2] Oto Luthar, *The Land Between: A History of Slovenia* (Frankfurt am Main: Peter Lang, 2008), p. 280.

[3] Mark Mazower, *The Balkans: From the End of Byzantium to the Present Day* (London: Phoenix, 2001), p. 126.

[4] Misha Glenny, *The Balkans 1804-2012: Nationalism, War and the Great Powers* (London: Granta, 2012), pp. 133-134.

[5] Tom Gallagher, *Outcast Europe: The Balkans, 1789-1989: From the Ottomans to Milošević,* (London: Routledge,

Along with the conflicts between empires and states, a number of events and movements within the Balkan countries themselves would affect the foundation of Yugoslavia. In June 1903, a group of Serb army plotters, led by Captain Dragutin Dimitrijević (otherwise known as Aspis), assassinated the pro-Austrian Serb King Alexander Obrenović and his wife in Belgrade, as well the Prime Minister.[6] The crown then passed to the Karađorđević family and King Pete I. The new monarch gave a free hand over government policy to the military while being more sympathetic to Russia. As a result, Serb policy developed in a more hostile fashion towards the Austro-Hungarian Empire.[7] Intrigue in Serbia, however, was not over. Aspis later founded the secret Black Hand organisation of Serb nationalists in 1911. The Black Hand would gain historical infamy with its role in starting the First World War and Gavrilo Princip was its notorious member. Macedonian underground groups were also active during the first years of the 20th century and launched an uprising in 1903, put down by 40,000 Ottoman troops.

2001), p. 31.

[6] Richard J. Evans, The Pursuit of Power: Europe 1815-1914 (London: Penguin, 2017), p. 691.

[7] Ibid, p. 691.

Драгутин Т. Димитријевић-Апис

Dragutin Dimitrijević

Aleksandar

Meanwhile, in the Ottoman Empire, a group of disgruntled military units and underground organisations, revolted in 1908. Known as the "Young Turk Revolution," the uprising was the beginning of the end of the empire and the rise of Turkish nationalism. To its neighbors, the Young Turk revolt was proof that the Ottomans were in weakened position, and Austria's response was to formally annex Bosnia and Herzegovina.[8] It would not be long before others attempted to fill the power vacuum.

The uncertainty in the Balkan region provided impetus for all the nationalist groups as the

---

[8] Misha Glenny, *The Balkans 1804-2012: Nationalism, War and the Great Powers* (London: Granta, 2012), pp. 218-219.

empires went into terminal decline, and the situation erupted in a number of conflicts in 1912 and 1913 that became known as the Balkan Wars. Albanian tribesmen occupied Skopje (the capital of today's Republic of Macedonia), providing the spark for others to move. In October 1912, Bulgaria, Greece, Montenegro, and Serbia all commenced hostilities, attempting to expand their territory.[9] Soon it was the Serbs that occupied Skopje. Meanwhile, Greek forces occupied the ancient port city of Salonika, pushing out the Ottomans after hundreds of years.

The fighting threatened to drag in the larger powers, and consequently the British convened a peace conference. The Treaty of London was signed in May 1913 to draw the map of the region, essentially without the Ottomans.[10] Soon afterwards, however, fighting resumed and Bulgaria gained land, confirmed in the Treaties of Bucharest and Constantinople.[11]

The wars had been relatively short in duration, but the modern military techniques had proven destructive, killing 200,000 men on all sides. As historian Richard J. Evans noted, "These wars were a portent of things to come."[12] The Balkan Wars also created a certain picture of the region in the minds of Western Europeans, especially as reports from the period described Balkan "barbarism" and particularism in the savagery undertaken by combatants.[13] It was a reputation that lasted the entire 20th century, and it was so powerful that outside powers tried to justify intervention in the Balkan conflicts of 1912-1913 through Christian "Just War Thinking," invoking a duty to prevent savagery.[14]

World War I

Following the 1903 coup that installed Karađorđević on the Serbian throne, the country had internalized an anti-Austrian foreign policy. One of the offshoots of this stance was the Black Hand organisation, set up by the 1903 conspirators. It has been assumed that the plot to assassinate the Austro-Hungarian heir to the Imperial Crown, Archduke Franz Ferdinand, was supported by the Serbian government, but the truth was probably more complex. The Black Hand was a nationalist Serb outfit with links to the country's military and the goal of expanding the boundaries of Serbia to include all ethnic Serbs. This would include ethnic Serbs who lived in other parts of the Balkans, including Bosnia-Herzegovina.

Gavrilo Princip himself was born in Bosnia, and though he later claimed to be a Yugoslav nationalist wanting to free the Slavic people from Austrian domination, it was no coincidence that Princip and his group of collaborators chose June 28, 1914 to assassinate Franz Ferdinand. That date was the anniversary of the Serbs' iconic battle, the 1389 Battle of Kosovo. The desire

---

[9] Richard J. Evans, The Pursuit of Power: Europe 1815-1914 (London: Penguin, 2017), p. 693.

[10] Ibid, p. 695.

[11] Ibid, p. 695.

[12] Ibid, p. 697.

[13] Eugene Michail, 'Western Attitudes to War in the Balkans and the Shifting Meanings of Violence, 1912-1991', *Journal of Contemporary History*, (47:219, 2012), pp. 219-241)), p. 220.

[14] Ibid, p. 222.

to maximize Serbia's land - essentially the Serbs' "Big Idea" - would come back to haunt the Yugoslav project at the end of the 20th century.

The world reacted with horror to the assassination of Franz Ferdinand and his wife Sophie, nowhere more so than throughout Austria-Hungary, where there was widespread rioting against innocent Serbian citizens living within the empire's borders. It is surmized that many of those displaced eventually made their way back across the border to Serbia as refugees, further inflaming sentiment against Austrians and making an already volatile situation that much worse. Expressions of horror and commiseration came in from Germany, France, Britain (although the public and the government's attention there were far more focused on the rapidly escalating crisis in Ireland, where the independence movement had turned violent), and even Austria's recent enemy, Italy. Russia also offered its condolences, which was quite hypocritical given that the Russian government was almost certainly aware of the Serbian plot.

Overwhelmingly, the Great Powers sided with Austria, and a joint Austro-Hungarian and German demand was presented to the Serbian government to commence an internal investigation into the assassination, but the Serbian Ministry of Foreign Affairs dismissed such a request out of hand, claiming that there was absolutely nothing to investigate. This further aggravated an already awkward situation.

In the wake of the investigation into the death of Franz Ferdinand and the resulting trial and sentences that followed, along with the verdict of the court inculpating Serbia for the murders, the Austro-Hungarian Empire ultimately issued a letter to Serbia which became known as the July Ultimatum. This inflammatory letter demanded that the Kingdom of Serbia repudiate in writing the acts of the terrorists intent on destabilizing the legitimacy of the Austro-Hungarian monarchy and their hold over Bosnia-Herzegovina, and it also reminded the Serbian government that it had bound itself to abide by the terms of the agreement ceding it to Austria-Hungary in the first place. The letter also listed 10 key points which Serbia was expected to accept within 48 hours, and it threatened retaliation in the case of non-compliance.

The points listed were as follows:

1.   Serbia must renounce all propaganda designed to inspire hatred towards Austria-Hungary and which might prove harmful to its territorial integrity.

2.   The Organization known as the People's Defence must be disbanded forthwith, along with all organizations of a similar ilk.

3.   All propaganda against Austria-Hungary published in public documents, including school textbooks, is to be eliminated forthwith.

4.   All officers and government officials named by the Austro-Hungarian government are to be removed from office immediately.

5.   Members of the Austro-Hungarian government will be dispatched immediately to Belgrade, where they are to be given every assistance in suppressing subversive movements.

6.   All those involved in Franz Ferdinand's assassination are to be brought to trial forthwith, with the assistance of police investigators from Austria-Hungary.

7.   Major Vojislav Tankosic and Milan Ciganovic, known participants in the assassination of the royal couple, are to be immediately arrested.

8.   The Serbian government must cease all collusion in the transportation of weapons and equipment across the Austro-Hungarian Border, dismissing and disciplining the Border Patrol officials at Sabac and Loznica, who abetted the Sarajevo conspirators.

9.   Provide suitable explanation to the Austro-Hungarian government with regards to the actions undertaken by certain Serbian officials, who have demonstrated an attitude of hostility in their negotiations with the Austrian government.

10.   Immediately notify the Austro-Hungarian government once these measures have been enacted.

The letter set off a frantic flurry of activity in Serbia, but not of the kind the Austro-Hungarians wanted, aside from those in office who were clearly spoiling for a fight. Serbia telegraphed to St Petersburg asking for support, which Russia promised in the event of a fight. Reassured, Serbia then mobilized its armed forces before sending a reply to the July Ultimatum that conceded both points 8 and 10 but rejected the remaining points. The Serbs disguized their explicit refusal with a wealth of diplomatic actions that did nothing to fool the Austro-Hungarian government. The response from the empire was swift; the Austro-Hungarian ambassador in Belgrade was recalled, and troops began to prepare in for mobilization.

A propaganda cartoon after the assassination that asserted "Serbia must die!"

The day after the Austro-Hungarian ambassador departed from Belgrade, a convoy of Serbian troops being transported down the Danube River by steamer drifted off course towards the Austro-Hungarian bank near Temes-Kubin, where the local garrison commander ordered shots fired into the air to discourage them from landing. He wisely avoided firing upon the boats, which might well have precipitated a full-scale crisis, but as it was, his level-headedness would be to no avail. Unfortunately, the report which reached Emperor Franz Joseph I in Vienna about this incident inaccurately portrayed the trifling affair as a bloody last-ditch skirmish, and Franz Joseph I responded by declaring war. The Austrian Army was brought forward to a state of full mobilization, and the allotted divisions moved forward to their position on the Serbian border.

This was the move that set the dominoes of war in motion. Russia and France immediately mobilized their armies in response to the Austro-Hungarian threat, as they were required to do so according to the terms of the Secret Treaty of 1892, which stated that any mobilization of members of the Triple Alliance must be met. The initial, limited mobilization by Austria-Hungary was followed by a full-scale Russian one, which in turn was followed by a full-scale German and Austro-Hungarian call-up, which in turn precipitated a French one and finally a British one. Thus, with a suddenness that startled even those who felt it was inevitable, the major European powers all found themselves at war.

Although there had been explicit displays of commiseration and sympathy for Austria and widespread condemnation of Serbia's actions in the immediate aftermath of Franz Ferdinand's assassination, the attitude of the great powers towards Austria as the notional aggrieved party became substantially chillier as Austria insisted on virtually bullying Serbia over the whole affair. The British Prime Minister, Asquith, complained in an official letter that Serbia had no hope of appeasing Austria diplomatically, and that the terms of the July Ultimatum would've been impossible to meet even if Serbia was willing to do so. Indeed, it appears as though such an exacting document had been drafted precisely because Serbia didn't have a hope of complying, even if they had so wished, and thus Austria-Hungary would be able to go to war and punish them properly for the outrage perpetrated against their royal family.

100 years removed from the assassination, it might be unfair to say that it caused World War I, but it certainly started it. Historians still debate whether the Great War would have occurred even if Franz Ferdinand and Sophie lived out their lives in peace and comfort, but many believe that while it might've come months or years down the road, it was inevitable. The tangled web of alliances at cross-purposes, the growing diplomatic tensions, the arms race, the belligerence of newly powerful states such as Germany, the interference in other sovereign countries' affairs, and the relentless politicking all pointed towards one tragic outcome.

As for the parties themselves, it's apparent that much of the blame can be shouldered by the Serbian government. To this day, it's still unclear how much the King and Prime Minister knew about the plots and actions carried out by Dimitrijević and his associates in the Black Hand, but they were obviously privy to the official communications that involved Dimitrijević in his capacity as the head of Serbian Military Intelligence. Furthermore, it was the Serbian government, not the Black Hand (which at that point was virtually synonymous with Dimitrijević and Military Intelligence in any case) that provided Princip, Grabež, Cubrilovic, and the other conspirators with their firearms, explosives, training, and the means to cross the border into Bosnia. The People's Defence, the clandestine group within Bosnia, had been almost completely taken over by Serbian Military Intelligence and was effectively acting as a shell organization. Government officials from several different agencies had colluded with the conspirators on many occasions, with the end result that on the day of the assassination, the assassins were in place, suitably organized, well-armed for their purpose, and ready for action. At the same time, there are strong indications that several officials within the Serbian government (with or without sanction from on high) attempted to warn their Austro-Hungarian counterparts of what was to come.

Another country that must bear a share of the blame is Russia. According to the confession given by Dimitrijević at the end of his 1917 trial in Salonika, Russia was fully aware of his activities, and he had no reason to lie at that point. Indeed, according to Dimitrijević, the Russian Military Attachè in Belgrade had guaranteed that Russia would stand with Serbia against Austria-Hungary in the event that the operation was compromised, and that he had received funds from Russia to carry out the assassination. An investigative journalist attempting to uncover the truth received a fairly unconvincing testimony from the Russian Military Attachè, who denied any involvement. The Russian Military Attachè claimed that his Assistant had been in charge during the period leading up to the assassination, and that Dimitrijević never apprized him of his plans or intentions. It has also been suggested that the Tsar, or at the very least the Prime Minister, were aware of a forthcoming attempt against Franz Ferdinand's life and were not opposed to it happening. Russia had a vested interest both in weakening the Austro-Hungarian Empire and in destabilizing its hold on the Balkans as this might well potentially give it access to the strategically invaluable Mediterranean ports without having to pass through the Turkish-controlled Bosphorus and Dardanelles straits, which hampered its attempts to increase its naval power outside of the Black Sea.

Even Austria-Hungary, despite being the aggrieved party, had a hand in what followed the assassination. The Austro-Hungarian military had resisted many attempts at pacification with Serbia, including policies advocated by Franz Ferdinand himself, and it continued to pursue a policy of aggressive saber-rattling. Furthermore, the Governor of Bosnia, Oskar Potiorek, was a rigid and stubborn individual who viewed Slavic patriots as a national security threat and ruthlessly punished them accordingly, further inflaming anti-Austrian sentiment in a newly created province that required the most delicate of management rather than hamfisted pacification attempts. His refusal to countenance the use of improperly dressed troops to shield Franz Ferdinand and his halting of the motorcade in a vulnerable position near the bank of the river were symptomatic of his stubbornness, and his decision to remain idle while Sarajevo tore apart the homes of hundreds of innocent Serbs is evidence of his poor character.

Ironically, one of the few people who had no blame in what was to come was Franz Ferdinand himself. A choleric individual with the typical Austrian aristocrat's condescending attitude towards the subordinate Hungarian population, he was nonetheless no more prejudiced than many during his time and a great deal less than most; after all, he married a woman from the Czech aristocracy who was beneath his station. On top of that, his attitude towards Serbia and the Slavic issue was remarkably conciliatory for someone in his position. He went to his death unwittingly even after bravely continuing his public appearance despite having a hand grenade hurled at him. It is unfortunate for Franz Ferdinand that his birth and position made him an ideal target, but as history and fate would have it, he was simply the right man in the wrong place at the wrong time.

World War I engulfed many parts of the world, and it is mostly remembered due to the trench warfare on the Western Front, but the Balkans experienced the war very differently. It was a more fluid war, and it fundamentally changed every aspect of life in the region. In some cases, fighting in the Balkans dragged on into the 1920s, while the populations were "exchanged" on the basis of nationality.

The future Yugoslav Republics were pitted against each other from 1914-1918. The Ottomans aligned with Germany and Austria, which included Croatia, Slovenia, and Bosnia and Herzegovina.[15] Serbia fought against the Central Powers along with Montenegro. Somewhat ironically, it would be Serbia that came out of the conflict in the strongest position.

The war would decimate the Austro-Hungarian and Ottoman Empires, but their armies were still significantly larger than any of the smaller Balkan states that formed Yugoslavia. Serbia fought stoutly against the Austrians, but attacks from both the north and the east forced the Serb army to retreat in 1915. Its soldiers went on a long march through Kosovo and Albania before taking refuge in Greece.[16] Serbian King Peter I formed a government-in-exile on the island of Corfu, while the Macedonian and Montenegrin forces joined the Serbs in retreat.

King Peter I

When Russia transformed as a result of the revolution in 1917 and sought an armistice shortly afterwards, it appeared that Serbia had lost its vital benefactor, but the war ended the following year with British, Italian, and French troops finally defeating the Germans, Austro-Hungarians, and Ottomans. Those Balkan countries that had aligned themselves with the Allied forces would certainly benefit when the post-war geopolitical compact was settled at Versailles.

With the old empires in tatters by the end of the war, and with Russia incapacitated by its revolution, British and French power now dominated in the Balkans. Both had huge overseas empires of their own and were keen to expand their influence in the wider region, from the Balkans to the Middle East and North Africa.

Crucially for the story of Yugoslavia, Britain and France both favored Serbia.[17] Some writers

---

[15] David Owen, *Balkan Odyssey* (London: Indigo, 1996), p. 7.
[16] Ibid, p. 7.
[17] Eugene Michail, 'Western Attitudes to War in the Balkans and the Shifting Meanings of Violence, 1912-1991',

have put this in the context of the romantic nationalists that came to prominence in the 19th century, based first on liberating the Greeks (*Philhellenism*) from the Ottoman Empire and then other Christian national movements in the region. Indeed, London was home to a number of exiled nationalist movements. The more likely reason for the British and French support was that the Serbs made up the largest contingent in the West Balkan area. Therefore, support for Serbia may have offered the larger powers their best hope of stability, and this morphed into support for a Serb-led Slavic state.

The Formation of Yugoslavia

There were very few people within the Balkans who backed a Yugoslav state before 1918.[18] The concept of a union of the different nationalities in the region was the brainchild of a limited group of thinkers, which ensured Yugoslavia was essentially a top-down project. The two key architects of the state were Nikola Pašić, a Serb, and Ante Trumbić, a Croat.[19] The pair set up the "Yugoslav National Committee" in Paris in 1915, and this culminated in the July 1917 "Corfu Declaration," which set out the basis of a Yugoslav state, or a Kingdom of Serbs, Croats and Slovenes as it was then known.[20] France and Britain became early supporters of the Yugoslav project, seeing it as a potential bulwark against previous foes. Some, but by no means all British and French policy-makers believed that a Southern Slav state could prevent further instability in the region, which had been so instrumental in causing the war in the first place.

Journal of Contemporary History, (47:219, 2012), pp. 219-241)), p. 220.

[18] Mark Mazower, *The Balkans: From the End of Byzantium to the Present Day* (London: Phoenix, 2001), p. 114.

[19] Robert Gerwarth, *The Vanquished: Why the First World War Failed to End, 1917-1923* (London: Allen Lane, 2016), p. 189.

[20] Ibid, p. 197.

Pašić

Nikola Pašić was already in his late 60s by the start of World War I and had a long career in Serbian politics behind him. Pašić was Prime Minister in 1914 when the Austrians presented him with the "July Ultimatum," and although he accepted most of its demands, Vienna concluded that the Serb government and the "Black Hand" were one and the same. In exile during the war, Pašić became the leading Serb negotiator for the idea of a unified Slav state. During his long career, Pašić was most adept at gaining and accumulating power. Coupled with the instincts of Serb nationalism, he may have seen the Yugoslav project as a means of extending its influence.[21]

Although he may not have been personally enthusiastic about the idea, he was faithful to the wishes of the Serbian regent, Alexander, who was. Pašić also believed a number of assurances

---

[21] Misha Glenny, *The Balkans 1804-2012: Nationalism, War and the Great Powers* (London: Granta, 2012), p. 369.

had been made to the Croats and Slovenes during the war, alluding to a security alliance that needed to be honored in forming a unified state.

Croat leader Ante Trumbić, born in 1864, may have been even more fervent in desiring a unified nation. During the war, Croatia was forced to fight with the Austrians, but Trumbić, leading the London-based Yugoslav National Committee, lobbied the Allied Powers to accept the idea of Yugoslavia after the end of the conflict.[22] On July 20, 1917, the Corfu Declaration was signed and laid the foundation for Trumbić and Pašić's state. Shortly after the end of the First World War, on December 1, 1918, a Kingdom of Serbs, Croats and Slovenes was declared. Several days earlier, Serbia had formed a separate union with its ally Montenegro.[23] The Great Powers left the final settling of the state's borders for the imminent Versailles Conference, to be held near Paris.

Trumbić

Even before the state's foundation, tensions began to simmer between the different

[22] David Owen, *Balkan Odyssey* (London: Indigo, 1996), p. 7.
[23] Dejan Djokic, 'Versailles and Yugoslavia: ninety years on', *Open Democracy*, 26 June 2009, https://www.opendemocracy.net/article/versailles-and-yugoslavia-ninety-years-on

nationalities. The Croats and Slovenes saw the benefits of a united Slav state in terms of security; having been occupied for centuries by the Austrians, they were now wary of an expansionist Italy, which, having been on the side of the victors during the First World War, now sought territorial recompense. In particular, the Italians were making a claim on parts of the Dalmatian Coast in Croatia. The pooling of resources could buttress Croatia and Slovenia against outside threats, and ultimately this was crucial in the acceptance of a unified state under Serbian leadership.[24]

Nevertheless, a key principle was left unresolved between Pašić and Trumbić that would repeatedly come back to haunt Yugoslavia. Trumbić and the Croats believed they were signing up for a loose federation in which the component republics, namely Croatia, would have significant autonomy. Pašić and the Serbs, however, favored a unitary and more centralized state, naturally led by the majority Serbs. This tension led to several constitutions, a number of revolts, and the collapse of the country altogether generations later.[25]

In modern history books, the Treaty of Versailles looms large. Ostensibly called to formalize the end of the war, the prominent decision-makers at Versailles sought to punish the aggressors in the war and to stabilize Europe, in order to prevent further conflagration. The conference has been interpreted in many ways, but it is most widely remembered today as punishing Germany so harshly that it inadvertently led to World War II.

Versailles also brought about the creation of a number of new states, including Yugoslavia. The three major players at Versailles were French Prime Minister Georges Clemenceau, British Prime Minister David Lloyd George, and American President Woodrow Wilson. President Wilson came to Versailles with a separate, although clearly related set of priorities. Having issued his famous "Fourteen Points" for ending the war in January 1918, Wilson put more emphasis on democratic accountability and self-determination. At Versailles, this meant that new states were formed while border territories were given the option, through plebiscites, of choosing whether to join one state or another.[26]

This also meant that numerous delegations arrived at Versailles putting forward their cases for national sovereignty. For Yugoslavia, Nikola Pašić and Ante Trumbić were there, as well as nationalists from the countries that would constitute the unified state. These included an obscure Croatian nationalist by the name of Ante Pavelić, who was opposed to the Yugoslav idea, believing it to be a "Greater Serbia" project.[27] Pavelić would become one of the most notorious

---

[24] Mark Mazower, *The Balkans: From the End of Byzantium to the Present Day* (London: Phoenix, 2001), p. 114, David Owen, *Balkan Odyssey* (London: Indigo, 1996), p. 7.

[25] Robert Gerwarth, *The Vanquished: Why the First World War Failed to End, 1917-1923* (London: Allen Lane, 2016), p. 198.

[26] Godfrey Hodgson, *People's Century: From the dawn of the century to the eve of the millennium* (Godalming: BBC Books, 1998), p. 80.

[27] Robert Gerwarth, *The Vanquished: Why the First World War Failed to End, 1917-1923* (London: Allen Lane, 2016), p. 189.

figures in the state's history.

Pavelić

One of the key problems for the architects of the post-war world in Versailles was that when Wilson's ideas came into contact with reality, sovereignty and self-determination for some was not inclusive for others. It would prove impossible to draw borders containing discreet national groups, and this was evident within the multinational Kingdom of Serbs, Croats and Slovenes. Despite the liberal, progressive rhetoric at Versailles, the new states clearly included minorities that either did not want to live in the new arrangement or would be persecuted by the majority group.

Czechoslovakia and the Kingdom of Serbs, Croats and Slovenes were among the new states that officially came into being on June 28, 1919, five years after Gavrilo Princip had assassinated

Franz Ferdinand in Sarajevo. In Yugoslavia's case, a better way of describing Versailles was that its creation was not opposed by the Great Powers.[28] Moreover, the young state still had border disputes with Italy and Romania which remained unsettled until the 1920s.[29]

As the dust settled after Versailles, the Yugoslav delegation returned home to start the serious business of building a new state from scratch. Due to its previous domination by different empires, not to mention its different languages, cultures, and traditions, the separate republics had quite different structures. Pašić was temporarily out of power in the new state, while Trumbić was appointed foreign minister. Serbian monarch King Peter I assumed power over the new country, while his son, Alexander, wielded influence behind the scenes as Regent.

Alexander I

The early formation of Yugoslavia was quite different from the federal version that emerged

[28] Dejan Djokic, 'Versailles and Yugoslavia: ninety years on', *Open Democracy*, 26 June 2009,
    https://www.opendemocracy.net/article/versailles-and-yugoslavia-ninety-years-on
[29] Ibid.

after 1945. It contained six customs areas, five currencies, four rail networks, three banking systems, and initially two seats of government in Belgrade and Zagreb.[30] The region was overwhelmingly an agricultural economy, as approximately 75% of the population still worked on the land.[31] The state was split into a number of provinces, which broadly speaking can be seen as Slovenia, Croatia, Serbia, Bosnia, and Montenegro.

The new state, despite being a multiethnic formulation, paid little attention to a number of other nationalities present in the region in 1918. These included ethnic Germans, Greeks, Turks, Hungarians, Romanians, and Albanians.[32] Although the politics of the Kingdom bore some semblance to its European contemporaries - for instance a Social Democratic party existed, as well as the Democratic Party - there were numerous ethnically based parties, such as the Serbian Radicals, the Croatian Peasant Party, and the Slovenian People's Party. The Croat Peasants, dominated by Stjepan Radić, were initially proponents of an agrarian socialism and Croat autonomy, while the Democrats were the major voices for a centralized state.

Radić

[30] David Owen, *Balkan Odyssey* (London: Indigo, 1996), p. 7.
[31] Misha Glenny, *The Balkans 1804-2012: Nationalism, War and the Great Powers* (London: Granta, 2012), p. 396.
[32] David Owen, *Balkan Odyssey* (London: Indigo, 1996), p. 7.

A Fragile Democracy

During the war, Tomáš Masaryk started to call for a separate Czech state, but he took a controversially pro-Western position during the conflict and was forced into exile. One of Masaryk's ongoing concerns was regarded how a tiny country would achieve security in a disputed, hostile neighbourhood dominated by much larger powers. Indeed, it was a question that would guide much of his external relations and policy, and Masaryk kept coming back to the same solution: close alliances if not joint sovereignty with similar nations. Thus, during his exile, Masaryk called upon the other small Slavic countries of Central Europe and Eastern Europe to join forces. In some places such as Poland, Masaryk failed to achieve anything concrete, but he did make contact and come to an arrangement with likeminded Slovaks. The Czechoslovak National Council was formed in 1916 in Paris, under the tutelage of Masaryk, Edvard Beneš (a Czech), and Milan Štefánik (a Slovak).

Masaryk

Beneš

Štefánik

The real boost for the idea of an independent Czechoslovakia came from President Woodrow Wilson. The United States had sat on the fence for much of the conflict until 1917, but unrestricted submarine warfare made it possible for the Americans to join the war on the side of the Entente (France, Britain and Russia). In January 1918, President Wilson outlined his war aims, commonly known as his "Fourteen Points," which called for post-war Europe to consist of independent states exercising national self-determination and sovereignty. Wilson had concluded that the hegemonic European empires were to blame for the outbreak of war, and his Fourteen Points would prevent this situation recurring. What Wilson either didn't acknowledge or didn't appreciate was that most of the proposed independent states were far from ethnically or nationally homogenous. Indeed, most contained several different minority groups, and some of those groups were substantial, such as the Sudeten Germans.

At the time, however, Wilson's announcement gave hope to the likes of Masaryk, Beneš and Štefánik, and shortly afterwards, in May 1918, the respective Czech and Slovak national delegations agreed to a union. France, Britain, and the United States then recognised the Czechoslovak National Council as the representatives of the Czech and Slovak peoples, and the Council established a provisional government in October 1918 as the First World War entered its last days of fighting.

Masaryk and Edvard Beneš declared the independence of Czechoslovakia on 28 October 1918. Masaryk was chosen as the state's first President on November 14, while Beneš became Foreign Minister, Štefánik became Minister of War (only to die in a plane crash the following year), and Karel Kramář, a conservative who had been jailed for treason during the First World War, became Prime Minister.

Kramář

The Versailles Peace Conference started in January 1919 and culminated that June. The new state of Czechoslovakia was essentially consolidated by the victors at Versailles and had a powerful backer in President Wilson. Britain and France also came out strongly in favor of the new state, which was represented by Beneš at the talks, and those two countries essentially became its guarantors after the dust of Versailles had settled and the Americans had retreated back into isolationism.[33]

Masaryk was proved right in his analysis that any Czech state would need allies and alliances, and this was partly embedded within the union, given that Czechoslovakia essentially combined two different nationalist groups (not to mention the Sudeten Germans). It also needed other supporters, namely European powers that would back up treaty obligations.

Tensions were inherent at the very birth of Czechoslovakia. The border in the east with Hungary was disputed, but as part of the empire with Austria, Hungary was one of the defeated countries in the war, so Czechoslovakia received the benefit of any doubt. In the northwest, however, the young country would face a much more difficult problem, because the Treaty of Versailles compelled Germany to cede parts of what it had previously considered parts of its Reich. The Germans reluctantly agreed since they were facing an invasion if they did not sign the treaty, which essentially presented them with a *fait accompli*. As a result, Czechoslovakia contained over three million ethnic Germans, over 20% of its population, and many of them resented being under the control of Prague, rather than Vienna or Berlin. In fact, the Sudeten Germans were represented at Versailles and pushed for secession from any Czechoslovakian state, but without a = potent sponsor, the Sudeten Germans lacked support.

Given Wilson's sponsorship and the support of Britain and France, it was inevitable that the architects of Czechoslovakia were orientated towards the West. As a result, the young country developed institutions in a liberal democratic manner. Under the leadership of Masaryk and Beneš, a constitution was written that ensured parliamentary democracy and the rule of law. Czech and Slovak were the official languages, and minority rights were explicitly secured. The security of the new country was underpinned by a new international organisation, the League of Nations.

The government, known as Czechoslovakia's "First Republic," had all sorts of problems in the 1920s and 1930s, many pertaining to ethnic minorities. However, the decades were prosperous, and the country's democracy survived, led by the "father of the nation," Tomáš Masaryk.[34] Out of all the countries created or established after the Great War, Czechoslovakia was widely

---

[33] Godfrey Hodgson, *People's Century: From the dawn of the century to the eve of the millennium* (Godalming: BBC Books, 1998)

[34] *Prague Morning*, "81 Years Ago Today, Tomas G. Masaryk Died", http://www.praguemorning.cz/81-years-ago-today-tomas-g-masaryk-died-kclvjTJiBd, [accessed 10 April 2019]

considered to have been the most successful. In this regard, it had some advantages, as the former empire had bequeathed its successor industrial capacity and the wherewithal to produce goods and exploit resources, particularly in Czech lands.

Elsewhere in Europe, however, the 1920s brought serious political and economic strife. Germany's Weimar Republic struggled to pay its huge war reparations, and it subsequently suffered the traumas of hyperinflation and political instability. The other new states succumbed at various stages to dictatorships and political and economic mismanagement.

Czechoslovakia appeared to be the one unalloyed triumph of the Versailles negotiations, but Masaryk and Beneš were from the very outset concerned about the external security of their state. Germany may have been dramatically weakened in the wake of the war, but it was still a huge country on Czechoslovakia's doorstep, and not an especially friendly one. The subsequent events have naturally focused on the Nazi takeover of Germany and Hitler's actions in Czechoslovakia, but Weimar-era policymakers were also very unhappy about the status quo.[35]

As a result, Czechoslovakia sought alliances to buttress its position, and the fear of an external threat did much to bind Czechs and Slovaks together. As one demonstration of this quest for security in the 1920s, Czechoslovakia formed the "Little Entente" with Yugoslavia and Romania.[36] This was reinforced by the support of France and Britain, which both achieved relative stability during the decade. Ironically, it was only when external threats were removed that the bonds between the Czechs and Slovaks quickly frayed.

By the early 1930s, Czechoslovakia had become one of the richest countries in the world, and a Czechoslovak nationality had been forged (though this was partly to ensure that the combined number of Czechs and Slovaks outweighed the number of Sudeten Germans in any statistics or census).[37] However, the global order established at Versailles was beginning to crumble by the early 1930s, and Czechoslovakia's neighbours struggled with the implications of the 1929 Wall Street Crash and the Great Depression. The environment was a breeding ground for political extremism and geopolitical grievance, and when Adolf Hitler took power in January 1933, Czechoslovakia was the only democracy left in Central Europe and Eastern Europe.

Furthermore, the instability spread to Czechoslovakia, and the integrity of the country was weakening. In Slovakia, an independence movement grew louder, the first signs that perhaps Czechoslovakia would not last forever. Before that could gather momentum, however, the country would lose its independence altogether.

---

[35] Godfrey Hodgson, *People's Century: From the dawn of the century to the eve of the millennium* (Godalming: BBC Books, 1998)

[36] Misha Glenny, *The Balkans 1804-2012: Nationalism, War and the Great Powers* (London: Granta, 2012)

[37] Godfrey Hodgson, *People's Century: From the dawn of the century to the eve of the millennium* (Godalming: BBC Books, 1998)

Immediate Instability in Yugoslavia

One of the first challenges for the new Yugoslav state was to pass a constitution. The document barely achieved parliamentary consent on June 28, 1921 after having been proposed the previous year. In fact, it achieved only a simple majority, as opposed to the 60% stipulated in the Corfu Declaration.[38] It became known as the "Vidovdan Constitution," as it shared the date of the famous remembrance of Serb national identity.

A new administrative structure was set out in the document, with 33 new Oblasts (provinces) essentially forming a unitary, Serb-led, centralized monarchy. Nationalists in the smaller non-Serb areas were outraged. For Croats and Slovenes, this was a betrayal of the agreements made during the First World War. Support for the new state weakened in its peripheral regions throughout the next two decades, and almost immediately, peasant groups violently opposed the 1921 constitution.[39] Indeed, the battle over the constitution paralyzed politics over the first half of the 1920s, with the main Croat nationalist leaders refusing to participate.

The dominant figures in the first phase of Yugoslavia were politicians such as Nikola Pašić and the Karađorđević monarchy. The Karađorđević family had been locked in a battle for influence in Serbia throughout the 19th century with the Obrenović family. The former was pro-Russian, while the latter was pro-Austrian, and each wanted to reduce the influence of the opposing power.

The 1903 coup that murdered the Obrenović king appeared to have settled the Serbian monarchy question, and King Peter I had been on the throne as Serbia gone through the successes and failures of World War I and the formation of the Kingdom of Serbs, Croats and Slovenes. Peter I now projected more Serb influence than had existed, in the Serbian nationalists' eyes, for hundreds of years.

It was Peter I's son, Alexander, however, who was the more committed supporter of a unified Yugoslav state of Southern Slavs. Alexander, then 32 years old, became king in August 1921 following the death of his father, and he would play a pivotal role in the historical development of Yugoslavia over the next decade. King Alexander I's erratic rule proved antagonistic to the ethnic minorities within the state, particularly the Croats, and this rivalry overshadowed the early years of the country. Croat nationalists were not the only minority to sour over the idea of Yugoslavia, as some of the most potent challenges to the new state were Macedonian underground groups.

The IMRO (Internal Macedonian Revolutionary Organization, the successor of the MRO) had already made its mark on Balkan history thanks to its campaign of improvized violence and subversion at the turn of the century. In a unified Yugoslavia, the Macedonians were clearly

---

[38] Misha Glenny, *The Balkans 1804-2012: Nationalism, War and the Great Powers* (London: Granta, 2012), p. 403.
[39] Mark Mazower, *The Balkans: From the End of Byzantium to the Present Day* (London: Phoenix, 2001), p. 114.

subjugated behind other nationalities, and the IMRO and other Macedonia underground groups such as the Macedonian Federative Organization (MFO) renewed their provocative activities. During the 1920s, the IMRO circulated rumours that Italy was about to invade, causing grave concern among Croats in particular.[40] The IMRO had a number of objectives, ranging from gaining separate autonomy within a Balkan Federation to being incorporated into the Bulgarian state.

The Kingdom of Serbs, Croats and Slovenes ostensibly managed to settle its boundary questions with the Treaty of Rapallo in November 1920. Located south of Genoa, the Rapallo document was signed by the Yugoslavs and Italy, settling the status of Dalmatia and Istria within Croatia. For the Croats, however, this was a bitter pill to swallow, as the Treaty proposed independent sovereignty over a number of cities in Istria and Dalmatia, including Rijeka (known as Fiume to Italians).[41] Nikola Pašić had disturbed the Croats in the Yugoslav delegation during the wartime negotiations with the Allied Powers through his potential willingness to sign over Croat and Slovene land to the Italians in return for land favored by Serb nationalists in Macedonia and Albania.[42] Indeed, as Prime Minister, Nikola Pašić formally signed these territories over to Benito Mussolini in January 1924, much to the dismay of Croats. Meanwhile the newly formed countries in the region – Yugoslavia, Czechoslovakia and Romania – formed the so-called "Little Entente," an alliance to improve their respective positions against the former imperial powers, in 1920.

Pašić had returned to office in 1921 and became the dominant figure in the first years of the nation. Although Yugoslavia was nominally democratic, these institutions never took root in the first decades of the state's existence.[43] Much was made of this in later years, but clearly democracy in the Balkans was relatively novel. Moreover, if voters simply supported parties of their own nationality, democracy was likely to be extremely difficult. The only idea that truly cut across the different ethnicities was socialism, and this would not gain broad support for awhile. In the 1920s, political parties found it difficult to appeal to several part of the nation.

Croat separatists such as Radić came in behind the Belgrade authorities for a time in the mid-1920s. The Croatian leader had been jailed in January 1925 on charges that his party had broken a 1920 law, the Obznana Decree, which had been initially designed to suppress the Communist Party. Shortly afterwards, however, Radić stunned his opponents and supporters alike by throwing his weight behind the Vidovdan Constitution. In fact, the Croatian Peasant Party leader came to an agreement with King Alexander I due to the threat posed to Croatian integrity by Mussolini's fascist Italy. The king realized he needed his country's two biggest parties to come to terms with each other if he was to achieve stability. Therefore, Radić instructed his nephew to

[40] Nada Boskovska, *Yugoslavia and Macedonia Before Tito: Between Repression and Integration* (London: IB Tauris, 2016)

[41] Misha Glenny, *The Balkans 1804-2012: Nationalism, War and the Great Powers* (London: Granta, 2012), p. 377.

[42] Ibid, pp. 369, 377.

[43] David Owen, *Balkan Odyssey* (London: Indigo, 1996), p. 7.

make a statement to the Belgrade parliament: "The Vidovdan Constitution exists here today de facto, this is a political fact of life, with the Karadjordjević (Karađorđević) dynasty as the head of the state. This is a fact which we accept unconditionally and with which we agree...Although it may look as though we have made concessions to our brothers, those brothers are the Serbian people and represent our joint future together."[44]

Radić was released from prison shortly after the declaration, and the development was a major breakthrough in the already fractious history of Yugoslavia. King Alexander I brokered a coalition agreement between the Serbian Radicals and Radić's Croatian Peasant Party, and for a time the country seemed to be moving into a new phase of peace and prosperity. The economies of major cities such as Zagreb and Belgrade appeared to boom.

The truce only lasted, however, until the next round of discord threatened to overwhelm the fragile state. Pašić resigned in 1926 due to a corruption scandal, and his son Rade was implicated in a number of graft allegations that became a point of constant criticism from the Croatian Peasant Party.[45]

Relations between the Serb Radicals and Croatian Peasant Party deteriorated after Pašić, a flawed politician but one who could at least claim to represent some continuity, resigned. The parliament, known as the Skupština, became home to almost daily shouting matches, intimidations, and squabbles which threatened to turn violent. Stjepan Radić himself had been threatened on several occasions by other parliamentarians.

On June 19, 1928, a member of the Serb Radicals, Puniša Račić, pulled out a revolver in the parliament and shot three Croatian Peasant Party MPs, including Radić. The Croat leader initially appeared to recover, but he died on August 8 of that year.[46] The assassinations caused outrage across the country, especially in Croatia. The government attempted to struggle on, but disputes only grew, and coalitions proved impossible to form.

On January 6, 1929, King Alexander I suspended the democracy and effectively seized power for himself as part of a monarchical dictatorship. Alexander renamed the Kingdom of Serbs, Croats and Slovenes in October 1929 to the more familiar Yugoslavia, loosely translated as Land of the Southern Slavs.

The king remained obsessed with the "Croat Question," and how to pacify the demands of Croat separatists while maintaining the integrity of the Yugoslav project. It is worth noting that the other nationalities did not always support Croat claims of Serb dominance. Indeed, the Slovene People's Party and the (Bosnian) Yugoslav Muslim Organization often supported Belgrade in the disputes with Zagreb in the 1920s.[47]

---

[44] Misha Glenny, *The Balkans 1804-2012: Nationalism, War and the Great Powers* (London: Granta, 2012), p. 405.
[45] Ibid, p. 407.
[46] Ibid, pp. 408-412.

Nonetheless, Croat nationalists were certainly developing greater animus to the Yugoslav state by the end of the decade. The controversy over the Vidovdan Constitution, territorial concessions to Italy, and the 1928 assassinations had provided much fuel to the separatist fire. The feeling held by Croat nationalists was that Yugoslavia was a Greater Serbian project that was either indifferent, or at worst hostile to Croat sentiments. Radić's funeral – acting as a locus of Croatian nationalism and grievance - was attended by hundreds of thousands, and the red and white chequered flag, subsequently synonymous with the Ustaše terrorist group, was brandished at the funeral for the first time.

Another Croat nationalist, Ante Pavelić, fled Yugoslavia in 1929, having contacted the IMRO. Pavelić had already established an underground Croat group, known as the Ustaše, from the acronym UHRO (Croatian Revolutionary Organisation). The Ustaše attracted emigres who were living in exile across Europe, particularly Austria, and started a campaign of violence and assassinations within Yugoslavia. Pavelić was tried and sentenced to death in Yugoslavia, but by this point he had fled into exile in Mussolini's Italy.[48] This suited Mussolini, who had come to power in 1922 and saw the possibility of splitting Yugoslavia and gaining greater regional influence for Italy.

Many more Yugoslavs would become sympathetic to groups such as the Ustaše and the IMRO after October 1929 and the Wall Street Crash. Although the crash took place in the United States, it impacted virtually every economy that participated in the global trading system. King Alexander I responded to the crisis in a number of ways, strengthening central (that is to say Serb) control over the economy. The national minorities in Yugoslavia believed that they suffered more economic pain than the majority Serbs, therefore intensifying the rivalries and animosities that had built up in the 1920s. The country was straining under the limits of the Gold Standard, and the level of its foreign trade declined.

King Alexander I had also reorganized the administrative structure of his country shortly after its name change to Yugoslavia. 33 Oblasts became nine new regions, or *banovinas*, and in 1931 he signed a new constitution that put executive power officially in the hands of the monarch. Democracy in Yugoslavia had been officially extinguished.

Alexander formed a separate autocratic tool for his decrees, called the "Court for the Protection of the State," which stifled any opposition to the king. The Court quickly arrested the two most prominent opposition politicians, Vladko Maček and Svetozar Pribićević. Maček had become leader of the Croatian Peasant Party after Stjepan Radić's assassination in 1928, and as a leading opponent of the king, he was jailed in 1933 for treason. Svetozar Pribićević, on the other hand, was a Serb from Croatia who strongly supported the idea of Yugoslavia. Pribićević had been a Democrat before setting up a splinter party, but, having changed his mind about a centralizing

---

[47] Misha Glenny, *The Balkans 1804-2012: Nationalism, War and the Great Powers* (London: Granta, 2012), p. 408.
[48] Ibid, p. 430.

approach, formed a political partnership with Croat nationalists such as Radić. He was jailed in 1929 but released in 1931 due to poor health. Pribićević became a leading critic of Alexander's dictatorship from exile in Paris before his death in 1936.

Extrajudicial killings were also prevalent. In February 1931, a leading Croatian intellectual who opposed Yugoslavia, Milan Šufflay, was murdered outside his home by members of the royalist Young Yugoslavia group. The murder provoked an international outcry.

Ante Pavelić, in exile in Italy, took more extreme positions during the 1930s.[49] His vision for an independent Croat state incorporated more and more of Yugoslavia. Pavelić was developing his own "Big Idea" of Croatia, as many Croats lived in Bosnia and Herzegovina as well as regions of Serbia. The Ustaše leader appealed to both Croat emigres and, most predominantly, peasants. In this respect he filled the space of the Croatian Peasant Party led by Radić and then Maček. In 1933, in *Principles of the Ustaše Movement*, Pavelić wrote, "The peasantry is not just the base and source of our life but alone contains the essence of the Croatian people and is, as such, the executive of all state power in the Croatian state." As a result, Pavelić could recruit ordinary Croats to his cause.

At the same time, he also kept links with other underground groups and it was to them he turned to initiate his most incendiary move against the Yugoslav state to date. Pavelić eventually contacted the Macedonian IMRO to plot the assassination of King Alexander I. Having settled on a plan, the IMRO assassins, led by Vlado Chernozemski and backed up by Croats, traveled through Hungary to Switzerland to France, where the king was due to attend a state visit as part of his country's Little Entente agreement. On October 9, 1934, King Alexander I arrived in Marseille, France and began his visit accompanied by the French Foreign Minister through the city in an open car. Chernozemski appeared from the crowd and shot the king twice, killing him.

The Price of Appeasement

Hitler's vision of Germany, which appealed to many Germans during the heady days of the later 1930s, centered on renewal and a return to Germany's glorious destiny. Disarmed, subjected to enormous war reparations, and deprived of their economically crucial Ruhr industrial territory, the Germans suffered a series of catastrophes that burned deeply into the national consciousness. Runaway inflation destroyed the German economy to the extent that near famines occurred shortly before Hitler's rise to power. Farmers attempting to keep their crops and starving city-dwellers desperate to survive engaged in actual gun-battles over grain and livestock in the German countryside. While several American-sponsored initiatives eventually set the German nation on the course to economic recovery, Hitler already controlled the government at that point and claimed that Germany owed her changes in fortune exclusively to him and his budding "Thousand Year Reich."

---

[49] Misha Glenny, *The Balkans 1804-2012: Nationalism, War and the Great Powers* (London: Granta, 2012), p. 433.

Hitler's refurbishment of the German army met with widespread approval by the populace, which was understandably weary of the helpless, inferior position imposed on them by the hated treaties ending World War I. Simultaneously, however, most Germans abhorred and dreaded the notion of a second major conflict involving their nation. For several years, therefore, the Fuhrer pretended to have peaceful intent. This pretense served not only to prevent early intervention by foreign powers, who tacitly recognized Germany's right to rearm to some extent, but also reassured German citizens alarmed at the prospect of renewed war. An expert juggler and manipulator, Hitler managed to appear "all things to all men," soothing war-weary Germans while holding out the promise of conquest and bloodshed to his aggressive Nazi followers. The conciliatory side of Hitler's act showed him as a restrained, peace-seeking statesman seeking no more than a prudent defense of Germany.

At the core of Hitler's policy lay the Four-Year Plan, overseen by Hermann Goering among others. This plan aimed to prepare Germany for war during the 1940s, clearly indicating the boundlessness of Hitler's ambitions, but intriguingly, these two leading Nazis diverged sharply regarding the Third Reich's future. Hitler wished not just to create Greater Germany but to achieve "Lebensraum," displacing, enslaving, or exterminating the Slavs to fill eastern Europe and Russia with his Teutonic "master race." Goering, on the other hand, envisioned an aggressive but far more realistic scheme. In his opinion, Hitler should build Greater Germany, then extend influence and domination into southeastern Europe via economic and diplomatic means rather than direct invasion. This would lay the groundwork for Germany as a superpower along the lines of the United States or Russia, based more on a militarily unassailable country with the overwhelming industrial and financial might to exert political influence globally.

To achieve this goal, Goering especially wanted to ensure an alliance with Britain, eschewing any steps that might prompt armed hostility from the English. Such a plan might even have succeeded, since the outside world would have perceived Germany as a grim and dictatorial but essentially rational superpower, rather than a berserk rogue state determined to conquer the world. Eventually, only Goering possessed the fortitude to tell Hitler his launch of a new world war represented a major error, and to ask him to reconsider.

That said, Goering was not the Fuhrer, and Hitler's program of building a "Greater Germany" – a territory to encompass all regions of Europe with majority German speakers, including Austria and portions of Czechoslovakia known as Sudetenland – commenced in earnest on March 7th, 1936. On this date, the Fuhrer sent 3,000 Reichswehr soldiers, supported by 30,000 more held in reserve, into the Rhineland area, a demilitarized zone created following World War I. The French remained inactive, thus permitting the Third Reich to consolidate its power over this first "recovered" territory. Given that the Rhineland formerly lay within Germany's borders, Paris likely felt unwilling to start a fresh conflagration over a region to which Germany possessed considerable claim.

Crucially for Hitler, Neville Chamberlain took the post of Prime Minister in May 1937. Viewing the Germans as an essentially civilized people and the Slavs as a barbaric horde outside the gates of Europe, he showed an inclination to cut the Nazis considerable slack. Chamberlain placed Nevile Henderson as his ambassador to the Third Reich, and he tended thereafter to place great reliance on his recommendations. As it would turn out, Ambassador Henderson proved to be something of an asset to Hitler in maintaining uneasy but good enough relations with Britain during the early stages of Nazi adventurism. Henderson expressed his views on Third Reich aggression quite frankly: "[T]he German is certainly more civilized than the Slav, and [...] also less potentially dangerous to British interests – One might even go so far as to assert that it is not even just to endeavor to prevent Germany from completing her unity or from being prepared for war against the Slav provided her preparations [...] reassure the British Empire that they are not simultaneously designed against it."

Though it was Hitler who gave the actual orders, the British and French – and Chamberlain in particular – bear some culpability for the Wehrmacht's eastward push in the ensuing years. Chamberlain signally failed to provide any concrete aid to democracies such as Poland and Czechoslovakia, rendering them less effective as a bulwark against future Soviet aggression and making German aggression against the Soviets almost inevitable.

Chamberlain

Hitler called a fateful meeting in the Berlin Reich Chancellery on November 5th, 1937. Beginning at 4:15 p.m. and lasting slightly more than four hours, the meeting involved the top brass of the Nazi military machine on land, sea, and in the air. The roll call included the Luftwaffe head and number two Nazi, Hermann Goering, as well as war minister Werner von Blomberg, foreign minister Konstantin von Neurath, the Fuhrer's personal military adjutant Friedrich Hossbach, naval chief Erich Raeder, and overall army commander Werner von Fritsch. Hitler concisely outlined his agenda for 1938: "'Our first objective must be to overthrow Czechoslovakia and Austria simultaneously to remove the threat to our flank in any possible operation against the West.' So the targets were to be the two states created by the Versailles peacemakers to keep Germany contained in central Europe. [...] when the time came, Hitler said, 'the descent upon the Czechs would have to be carried out at lightning speed.'"

Meanwhile, there was a sharp divide over how to handle these developments among British officials. The majority faction, led by Chamberlain and Lord Halifax (then Lord President of the Council and soon to be Foreign Secretary) favored appeasement of Hitler and the Third Reich. The minority, spearheaded by Foreign Secretary Anthony Eden, believed in the League of Nations and called for strict opposition to German aggression, even if that led to armed conflict. In the end, the overt emergence of Hitler's threatening designs upon Austria strengthened the position of the appeasement faction headed by Chamberlain. Far from heeding Eden's warnings that yielding to the Third Reich's demands would make war more, not less, likely, the other British leaders came to view the Foreign Secretary as a nuisance.

In the wake of the Nazi acquisition of Austria, a decisive split between Chamberlain and Winston Churchill began. Churchill wanted to issue an ultimatum to Hitler that any additional invasions on his part would lead to war with England. Churchill also wished to prepare for just such an eventuality in order to carry out the threat if Hitler refused to stop his depredations. Chamberlain, on the other hand, confined himself to almost maternal remonstrances towards the German dictator. For example, on one occasion, he "informed his sister that he would tell the Fuhrer that 'it is no use crying over spilt milk and what we have to do now is consider how we can restore the confidence you have shattered.'" Lord Halifax, the Foreign Secretary, naturally backed up Chamberlain's position. Both men had a vague notion that Germany needed to be stopped diplomatically, but they had no concept of how to achieve this in practice. As if to weaken their own bargaining position more, the British government sharply reduced their military spending immediately following Hitler's annexation of Austria. The Germans took note of this and went ahead with preparations to move next on Czechoslovakia.

The high population of ethnic Germans living in western Czechoslovakia provided Hitler with the pretext he needed to incorporate these areas into his growing Nazi empire. His success at taking the Rhineland and Austria without active opposition by the Allies in general, and Britain in particular, encouraged him to indulge his ambitions with less and less restraint. Indeed, the British attitude towards Czechoslovakia indicated that they did not exactly stand ready to fight and die for that eastern European country. If anything, the British government viewed Czechoslovakia as scarcely more than a figment, and a highly annoying one at that. "Czechoslovakia, with its disgruntled minorities of Germans, Poles, Ruthenians, and Magyars, seemed to reflect in microcosm the difficulties of that earlier 'ramshackle' state. Nevile Henderson, who referred to the Czechs as 'those blasted Czechs,' had spoken to people in England, so he maintained, who regarded Czechoslovakia as a new variety of interesting flower. A colleague of his, he later recorded, had begun a dispatch to London: 'There is no such thing as Czechoslovakia.'"

These sentiments are made all the more ironic by the fact that in 1938, Czechoslovakia remained as a single beacon of democratic society among a miasmal bog of fascist and pseudo-fascist states. This political liberty provided one reason for Hitler's desire to seize the small but prosperous nation; its democratic success gave the lie to his propagandist declaration that the only alternative to his fascist totalitarianism was the even worse despotism of the Soviet and communist nations.

Other reasons weighed yet more heavily in the balance. Czechoslovakia's mountainous, heavily fortified western boundary presented a strategic obstacle to the Wehrmacht's freedom of maneuver in extending the Reich eastward. Furthermore, the Czechs possessed a large, modern industrial base. This juicy prize, added to Germany's already formidable manufacturing capabilities, made even more rapid armament of the Wehrmacht feasible, and it would make the destruction of the Soviet Union a realistic possibility in the absence of British and American interference.

Helping Hitler's cause, German majorities existed in many western Czech border regions, with more than 50% of the population speaking the German language and professing Teutonic rather than Czechoslovak loyalties in 1937 and 1938. The world financial crises of the 1930s hit these Sudeten Germans particularly hard, and though the central government attempted to offer relief, the economic impact grew too overwhelming to counter with various policies. A secession movement arose under a former teacher named Konrad Henlein, and, though not Nazi in orientation, it adopted many tactics familiar to the brownshirts of the SA. The use of violence and intimidation at the polls became commonplace, meaning that Henlein could muster a reliable 75% majority vote in most Sudeten districts with large German populations.

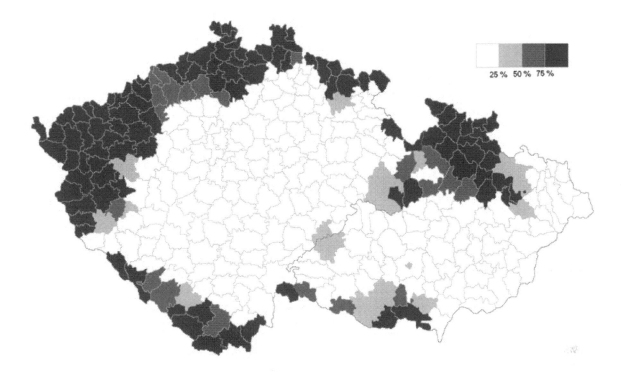

A map of parts of Czechoslovakia with heavy German ethnicity

Henlein

The Sudetenland Germans' attraction to joining the Third Reich centered on economic rather than ideological factors. Germany's economic recovery presented a tempting vision of business and employment to the reeling Sudetenland workers. Hitler's weaponry manufactures created many high-paying jobs in the Third Reich, and the Sudeten Germans longed for a slice of that newfound affluence.

Naturally, Hitler remained ready and willing to manufacture pretexts for intervention. The May Crisis of 1938, largely a product of hysterical rumors, exercised major influence over the actions of Chamberlain and his Cabinet later in 1938. At the outset, Czechoslovak police allegedly shot and killed two German motorcyclists in the Sudetenland. More crucially, the Wehrmacht held springtime exercises near the Czechoslovakian border, generating vast alarm in both Paris and London. Though Hitler intended to seize Czechoslovakia by military force later that year, the maneuvers that catalyzed such international frenzy had nothing to do with this scheme, as the Nazis simply did not consider themselves ready to take Czech territory in late spring or early summer. The exercises represented a coincidence, a long pre-planned martial exercise with no ulterior motive which happened to coincide with the worst suspicions of those nervously watching the actions of Nazi Germany.

The British initially warned the Germans not to attack Czechoslovakia, coming very close to stating that they would intervene militarily should combat erupt. Thus, when the attack failed to materialize (due to the fact that Germans never intended their maneuvers to end with a May border crossing) the English government ascribed the absence of an attack to their own warnings. However, far from bolstering their confidence, this mistaken interpretation terrified them into future inaction. "The prime minister confided to his sister Ida that 'the more I hear about last weekend the more I feel what a damned close-run thing it was.' Chamberlain's brief flirtation with warnings to Germany was over. Even Halifax was chastened by his own boldness […] On May 22, the day after Halifax had sent his warning to Hitler, he telegraphed the French that they could not count on British support in the event of war with Germany."

Further exacerbating the problem, the English continued to view the Czechs with contempt bordering on hostility. In the *Daily Mail*, Lord Rothermere spoke for his fellow government officials when he declared coldly that "Czechoslovakia is not of the remotest concern to us." He added that if "France likes to burn her fingers there, that is a matter for France." Around the same time, the top men in Chamberlain's government expressed their hatred even more openly: "At the May 22 Cabinet meeting, reported Cadogan, the Cabinet was 'quite sensible – and anti-Czech.' In the minds of the British leaders, the attempts by this small nation to preserve their national integrity were simply irritants in the way of great-power diplomacy. Significantly, the Cabinet was, at this critical point, 'anti-Czech' rather than 'anti-Nazi'; its venom was reserved for the victim not the perpetrator of the crime."

With these moves, Hitler and Chamberlain both set the stage for the Munich Agreement of

1938 and Britain's betrayal of Czechoslovakia. The Fuhrer thirsted for conquest, carried forward by faith in the Wehrmacht's fighting abilities and the Lebensraum concept that "lesser races" should be exterminated in tens or hundreds of millions to make space for a population explosion among Germans. Hitler showed himself willing to mouth platitudes to keep foreign pressure or hostility in abeyance as long as possible, even though he had no use for peace and did not intend to halt his aggression in the foreseeable future.

While aggression compelled Hitler, fear and delusion ruled Chamberlain, to the extent that the British Prime Minister convinced himself avoiding war at any price was the chief imperative of his office. Simultaneously, he betrayed his lack of faith in democracy by tacitly believing only fascist dictatorship could prevent the spread of communist violence into Europe.

All the while, the Sudeten German Party in Czechoslovakia received a steady stream of Nazi funding to assure that they remained a thorn in the Czech government's side. Despite his avowed intention of "wiping Czechoslovakia from the map," Hitler proceeded with some caution; the Czech army mustered 31 divisions and, though weaker than Germany's forces, possessed a moderate level of professionalism and decent equipment. Furthermore, the Sudetenland regions provided a naturally defensible frontier with their rugged landscape.

Czech soldiers in the Sudetenland in 1938

As the summer passed, Britain considered ways of coercing the Czechs into cooperating with Hitler's Sudetenland plans in order to preserve good relations between Germany and England.

The British sent Lord Runciman to Czechoslovakia in late July to attempt negotiation of a settlement between the Sudeten Germans and the Czechoslovak central government, and though Runciman did his best, with perhaps more of a bias towards the Germans than his avowed impartiality made decent, his mission proved futile. In fact, it appears to have been a sort of public relations stunt by the British government, with Runciman a luckless dupe whom the Cabinet never intended to achieve anything concrete. The Germans ignored Runciman as though he did not exist, while Chamberlain contemptuously carried out separate negotiations with the Sudeten German Party and the Third Reich without bothering to consult with Runciman.

Runciman

The Germans and Chamberlain continued to figuratively pat one another's backs throughout August. The Fuhrer stated that Germany and England represented European civilization's two pillars, while the British representatives told the German strongman that it would be a woeful situation if the world's two foremost "white races" butchered each other in a fresh war. In their private memorandums to one another, the British leaders continued to heap scorn on Czechoslovakia and dismiss the country as useless, all but talking themselves into justifying the coming betrayal of the Munich agreement.

Despite the Czechs' willingness to negotiate during August, the Sudeten Germans remained intransigent. The month also witnessed the mustering of considerable Wehrmacht forces ominously close to the Czechoslovakian border.

In September 1938, Chamberlain decided that only extraordinary measures could prevent the outbreak of another war, so he took the unprecedented step of flying repeatedly to Germany to negotiate face-to-face with Hitler. The French, now led by Édouard Daladier, expressed some disgruntlement at the bilateral nature of Chamberlain's negotiations, as they had hoped for a trilateral council to decide the future. Nevertheless, Chamberlain went ahead and landed at Munich airport, where he was met by Nevile Henderson, the British emissary with a singular distaste for the Czechs. Chamberlain met Henderson's solicitous inquiries about his condition following the long flight with the confident assertion "I'm tough and wiry."

Shortly into meeting with Chamberlain, Hitler stated unequivocally that the Sudetenland must be removed from Czechoslovakia immediately and incorporated into Germany. Chamberlain immediately stated that he conceded the point "in principle," but that the Cabinet would need to be consulted first. Of course, since the Cabinet essentially rubber-stamped the Prime Minister's decisions, this statement was tantamount to Chamberlain conceding that Hitler could take the Sudetenland, all within the first hour of negotiations. Over the course of the discussion, Chamberlain also indicated he had no objection to Germany attacking Russia.

The day after Chamberlain's first meeting with Hitler, Czech President Beneš made the horrifying discovery that the British had given away the Sudetenland to Germany without even bothering to consult or even notify him. Humiliated but helpless, the Czech leader protested, only to have the British respond by threatening to abandon the Czechs entirely to the mercy of the Third Reich (something that would eventually happen). Powerless before this threat, Beneš agreed to allow the Sudeten Germans to carry out a referendum regarding whether they wanted to secede from Czechoslovakia and merge with the Third Reich.

Chamberlain's second meeting with Hitler occurred on September 21st and 22nd, 1938, and this time Hitler chose the posh Petersberg Hotel as the venue for the negotiations. Chamberlain expected a cordial meeting with the Fuhrer, operating under the mistaken assumption that the first meeting resolved most of the difficulties. Instead, Hitler went on the attack again, startling the Prime Minister. The Fuhrer, a practiced predator and a man skilled at dominating others, clearly sensed weakness in Chamberlain and closed in for the metaphorical kill.

This time, Hitler declared that the Sudetenland referendum was inadequate because it would require too much time, and that the Czechs must transfer control over the Sudeten regions immediately or he would repudiate the deal. Even Chamberlain balked slightly at this, since Hitler appeared to be demanding massive concessions and offering absolutely nothing in return.

Chamberlain intended to sell out the Czechs, but he wanted something of value, like an agreement that the Germans would not attack France, Britain, or any of the possessions of the British Empire.

Hitler sensed he had gone too far in asking for surrender of the Czechs without offering a quid pro quo, so accordingly, he approached Chamberlain at 2:00 a.m. on September 23rd, minutes before the British leader left to catch his airplane back to Britain. Dr. Paul Schmidt, who recorded the meetings with considerable accuracy, reported, "Chamberlain and Hitler took leave from one another in a completely friendly tone after having had, with my assistance, an eye to eye conversation. […] Hitler thanked Chamberlain for his efforts for peace. Hitler also spoke about a German-Anglo rapprochement and cooperation. […] He went back to his old tune: 'Between us there should be no conflict,' he told Chamberlain, 'we will not stand in the way of your pursuit of your non-European interests and you may without harm let us have a free hand on the European continent in Central and South-East Europe.'"

After that, Chamberlain left in an exuberant mood, feeling that he had gained exactly what he longed for: permanent peace between Germany and England. He had casually carved up the world between the two nations, breezily giving away Czechoslovakia and Eastern Europe to the Reich in exchange for a mere promise that Hitler would never interfere in British affairs. Upon his return to Britain, Chamberlain concealed Hitler's statements, instead providing a vague summary indicating that the Fuhrer only wished to acquire a few minor territories with ethnic German majorities. He made no mention of the German dictator's intention to expand boundlessly eastward in pursuit of Lebensraum, despite having been fully apprised of this by Hitler.

Finally, the British drew up a timetable on September 27th, 1938 that it hoped would appease both the Czechs and the Germans. This plan envisaged German occupation of two small territories outside the Czech fortification lines by October 1st, while British, Czech, and German representatives would meet in the Sudetenland on October 3rd to decide what additional Sudeten areas would be fast-tracked for handover to the Germans. On October 10th, German soldiers would enter the areas earmarked between October 3-9 by this trilateral group, and later in October, Germany, England, France, and Czechoslovakia would arrange a full-scale negotiation to finalize agreements and create a new, stable, independent Czechoslovakia without the transferred Sudetenland territories.

Though Hitler did not agree to this plan immediately, he postponed any other operations against Czech territory until he had time to speak again with Chamberlain. Thus, the British Prime Minister, the Fuhrer, the Frenchman Daladier, and Mussolini gathered in Munich on September 29th, 1938, to decide the fate of Czechoslovakia. France, Britain, Germany, and Italy did not see fit to invite the Czechs to the meeting; Chamberlain mentioned the notion obliquely at one point, but when Hitler demurred, the Prime Minister meekly accepted his decision.

A picture of Chamberlain, Daladier, Hitler, Mussolini, and Galeazzo Ciano taken just before the Munich Agreement was signed

Chamberlain's most famous critic, Winston Churchill, didn't mince words when it came to expressing his disgust with the deal: "We have suffered a total and unmitigated defeat ... you will find that in a period of time which may be measured by years, but may be measured by months, Czechoslovakia will be engulfed in the Nazi régime. We are in the presence of a disaster of the first magnitude ... we have sustained a defeat without a war, the consequences of which will travel far with us along our road ... we have passed an awful milestone in our history, when the whole equilibrium of Europe has been deranged, and that the terrible words have for the time being been pronounced against the Western democracies: 'Thou art weighed in the balance and found wanting'. And do not suppose that this is the end. This is only the beginning of the reckoning. This is only the first sip, the first foretaste of a bitter cup which will be proffered to us year by year unless by a supreme recovery of moral health and martial vigour, we arise again and take our stand for freedom as in the olden time."

For his part, in the wake of Munich, Hitler didn't even pretend to respect Chamberlain or the process that brought about the agreement. At one point, he told people around him, "Gentlemen, this has been my first international conference and I can assure you that it will be my last" On another occasion, Hitler said of Chamberlain, "If ever that silly old man comes interfering here again with his umbrella, I'll kick him downstairs and jump on his stomach in front of the photographers."

In the days after Munich, the Wehrmacht swarmed across the border into the Sudetenland, while the Czech army grudgingly fell back from their mountain positions and fortifications. 34 divisions of troops retreated from a formidable defensive line without firing a shot, and 175,000 ordinary people fled as well, hoping to steer clear of German control. The Czechs harbored few illusions about Hitler's character or the nature of Nazi Germany's culture and society; 50,000 more soon followed the initial panicked exodus.

A picture of Czechs leaving border lands taken by Germany

Conversely, the Sudeten Germans greeted the Wehrmacht with screaming enthusiasm, brandishing the emblems of fascism and showering the soldiers with bouquets of late-blooming flowers. The French, paradoxically, celebrated the Munich Agreement and the occupation of the Sudetenland also, to the astonishment of the American journalist William Shirer, who was in Paris on October 8th and wrote, "Paris a frightful place, completely surrendered to defeatism with no inkling of what has happened to France. At Fouquet's, at Maxim's, fat bankers and businessmen, toasting Peace with rivers of champagne. But even the waiters, taxi-drivers, who used to be sound, gushing about how wonderful it is that war has been avoided […] The guts of France – France of the Marne and Verdun – where are they?"

A picture of Sudeten Germans welcoming the arrival of German soldiers in the Sudetenland

Germany's territorial gains in Czechoslovakia represented far more than a mere slice of real estate; the regions that contained large numbers of ethnic Germans were home to Czechoslovakia's border mountain ranges and its formidable fortifications. Thus, the Munich Agreement stripped away the country's hard outer shell and exposed its defenseless inner territories. The entire process had the effect of opening a bank vault's doors to a robber and then expecting the robber not to touch the money inside it. Not surprisingly, the Nazis went further than the Munich Agreement permitted, though they stopped short of taking over Czechoslovakia totally. The Gestapo, swarming into the country like dark locusts, arrested over 10,000 people known or suspected to have anti-Nazi opinions and moved them to the concentration camps. A decree from Hitler fired 50,000 Czechs in the Sudetenland from their jobs and gave them to Germans instead, while the Nazis simultaneously banned the Czech language in those regions they controlled.

Exceeding the terms of the Munich Agreement from the start, the Third Reich carved off two long strips of territory, giving one to Poland and another to Hungary. The Kristallnacht violence against Jews on November 9-10, 1938 also extended into the newly taken Sudeten territories, cementing Hitler's policy of hate as an official cultural characteristic of ethnic Germans both inside and outside Germany's boundaries. Through it all, Chamberlain responded to this outrage in typical fashion: "'Oh, what tedious people these Germans can be!' said Neville Chamberlain when he read the reports of the anti-Jewish riots and the measures which followed. 'Just when we were beginning to make a little progress!'"

A map depicting the breakup of Czechoslovakia in the wake of the agreement

Meanwhile, the Germans continued to consolidate their position over the winter, and the Slovaks, ironically, provided the impetus for losing what little independence they themselves enjoyed. Seeing the Czechs weakened by the German seizure of the Sudetenland, they revolted against the central government and appealed to the Nazis for aid, which gave Germany the pretext to put the surviving fragments of Czechoslovakia out of their misery in early spring 1939.

In yet another typical negotiation session, Hitler targeted Czech leader Emil Hacha, an ailing man in his 60s. One writer described the scene: "Just like Schuschnigg before him, Hácha was kept waiting far into the night (while Hitler watched a popular film), then was mercilessly bullied […] German troops were already on the move, said Hitler. When Goring added that German bombers would be dropping their payloads on Prague within a few hours, the elderly, sick Czech President fainted."

Hacha, Hitler, and Goering meeting in 1939

In response to the threats, Hacha signed over control of Czechoslovakia to Hitler on March 15th, 1939. He also called the Prague and ordered his army to refrain from firing on the Wehrmacht as they swept forward to complete their conquest. The Czechs stood down, knowing their position to be utterly hopeless. Czechoslovakia became a Reich Protectorate under the control of Reinhard Heydrich, the infamous Blonde Beast.

Heydrich

The Nazi Invasion and Occupation

King Alexander I's death shocked a Yugoslav public already disturbed by decades of violence, and 500,000 attended Alexander's funeral. The monarchy then passed to Alexander's son, Peter II, but since he was only 11 years old, power transferred to a regent. Alexander's cousin, Prince Paul, was a far more conciliatory figure than Alexander, relaxing censorship and the political strictures of the dictatorship period. He attempted to reform the country from 1934, in particular, by offering Croats more autonomy.[50] Paul was described as a Yugoslav ruler, rather than

---

[50] David Owen, *Balkan Odyssey* (London: Indigo, 1996), p. 8.

adhering to the pro-Serb outlook of his predecessors, but even his more relaxed approach could not satisfy the growing animosity between Serbs and Croats. In fact, the promise of more autonomy only managed to increase the squabbling between Yugoslavia's two largest nationalities.

Prince Paul

Peter II

In 1938 Paul appointed a Prime Minister, Dragiša Cvetković, and then the following year, he made Vladko Maček Vice Premier in a final attempt to resolve the tension between Croats and Serbs. Elections were held in 1938 and won by the Yugoslav Radical Union with 54% of the vote, while Maček's United Opposition Party received 45%. In August 1939, the Cvetković–Maček Agreement was signed, forming a Croatian *banovina* with greater autonomy and powers.

Ultimately, it would be to no avail, because Yugoslavia was hurtling towards nationalist violence and authoritarianism far worse than anything the country had experienced in its short history.

The politics of Europe changed rapidly during the 1930s. Many countries abandoned democracy while political parties, and voters, moved towards the extremes of fascism and communism. In Yugoslavia this trend was particularly fraught due to the many different nationalities. A shift to fascist politics was likely to pose problems for ethnic, religious and national minorities. Meanwhile, a charismatic socialist named Josip Broz, now known as Tito, was making his ways through the ranks of the Yugoslav Communist Party.

Yugoslavia had come into existence, in geopolitical terms, through support from the major democratic powers at the end of the First World War. Britain and France, and to a lesser extent the United States, had been strong supporters of the South Slav state idea.[51] The Americans, however, had moved to an isolationist foreign policy after the incapacitation of President Wilson. Washington even failed to support the League of Nations in Geneva despite the institution being the brainchild of Wilson himself. Nevertheless, Britain and France still attempted to back the post-Versailles internationalist world order they had constructed well into the 1920s. Democracy, sovereignty and self-determination were the keystones of this order.

The Wall Street Crash destroyed more than the world's financial system, because the Great Depression upended the political arrangements in many countries. The downturn led to extreme insecurity, in terms of income, jobs, and even food, while authoritarian politicians offered stability, even at the cost of political suppression. As politics in much of Europe drifted towards the extremes of fascism and communism, dictatorships emerged across the continent. Many of these regimes would exploit class or ethnic divisions as tools of consolidating or sustaining their power, and this created unique dangers for a number of countries, particularly those with significant ethnic or religious minorities. The Treaty of Versailles, despite its noble intentions, had redrawn the barriers of a post-imperial Europe and included numerous linguistic, religious and national minorities within a new "nation-state." In the hands of a strongman, like Adolf Hitler, these minorities could be exploited to suit a wider agenda. The large German-speaking minority of Czechoslovakia, for instance, was invoked as a reason for territorial annexation, and the Jewish minority within Germany itself was remorselessly persecuted and characterized as outsiders who did not fit the Nazis' views of eugenics and "racial purity."

The same trends were observed in Yugoslavia. King Alexander I's abandonment of democracy caused a loss of support from Britain and France as liberals in these democracies concluded that the Balkan states had inherent authoritarian tendencies.[52] At the same time, ethnic rivalries

---

[51] Eugene Michail, 'Western Attitudes to War in the Balkans and the Shifting Meanings of Violence, 1912-1991', *Journal of Contemporary History*, (47:219, 2012, pp. 219-241), p. 230.
[52] Ibid, p. 231.

increased over the decade, particularly between Serbs and Croats. In many ways, the trends of the 1930s were uniquely dangerous when applied to Yugoslavia since the country was a fragile multiethnic state already beset with national rivalries. It was even more vulnerable to the forces of violent ethno-nationalism than its contemporaries. In fact, Yugoslavia would experience both extremes, with fascism in power during the Second World War and communism taking root after 1945.

The Little Entente alliance of Yugoslavia, Czechoslovakia and Romania was still in operation during the 1930s. Its "Treaty of Friendship," initially signed in 1922, was extended in 1927, 1932, and 1937. The pooled weight of the initiative, however, proved too weak to resist the more powerful countries. Czechoslovakia was dismantled by the Nazis in 1938 and 1939, and with that the Little Entente no longer functioned. Moreover, the democratic powers, Britain and France, abandoned Czechoslovakia at the 1938 Munich Conference. The Allies were desperate to avoid another continental war with Germany, but also there was some sympathy to German claims that the Treaty of Versailles had imposed unfair conditions on the country and marginalized many ethnic Germans. If Britain and France were willing to disengage with Czechoslovakia, they were likely to do the same with Yugoslavia, particularly as Belgrade had eschewed democracy in 1929.

Once it was clear that these friends would not come to the aid of its allies, Yugoslavia was left exposed to interference from the fascist states. In Yugoslavia, however, it was the Italian threat that most concerned its rulers. By the end of the decade, Belgrade was becoming increasingly concerned about its geopolitical position and security. As a result, Belgrade sought alliances to secure its status, and unfortunately, Prince Paul decided to approach Nazi Germany as a potential protector.[53] Back in 1934, Hermann Göring had attended King Alexander I's funeral and offered the country its diplomatic support. Göring had promised, "Germany will never support any activity…that aims at the break-up of Yugoslavia."[54] These words were to prove wholly false.

Prince Paul visited Hitler in 1939 to garner support for his fragile state, as well as to pay his compliments to the Europe's most powerful leader. Paul's visit appeared to have paid off, and he now felt more secure in the dangerous geopolitical environment. That year, German troops marched into Czechoslovakia and annexed the rest of the territory left over from the 1938 Munich Conference. In September, Germany invaded Poland, which instigated a response from Britain and France and started World War II.

Initially, it appeared that Yugoslavia might somehow be insulated from the conflict despite the dangerous friendship Ante Pavelić had with Benito Mussolini and the Ustaše's activities. After all, Göring and then Hitler had apparently given Paul security assurances, and Yugoslavia had declared its neutrality in 1939 despite the fact Paul was favourable to the Allies, assisting both

---

[53] Brendan Simms, *Europe: The Struggle for Supremacy 1453 to the Present* (London: Penguin, 2014), p. 358.
[54] Misha Glenny, *The Balkans 1804-2012: Nationalism, War and the Great Powers* (London: Granta, 2012), p. 436.

Greece and France in the face of the fascist powers.

However, the situation quickly changed. The Nazis overran Belgium and France in the summer of 1940 and suddenly controlled most of Europe. Hitler's plans and ambitions then turned east, and in 1941 he had the Soviet Union in his sights. Yugoslavia, despite his earlier promises, would become a pawn in a far larger conflagration.

With Nazi power at its zenith, the fascist powers turned their attention to the Balkans in early 1941. They did this through the vehicle of the "Tripartite Pact," an agreement that unified Germany, Japan and Italy the Axis Powers in September 1940. Later that, year a number of countries had joined the pact, including Hungary and Romania, and in March 1941, Bulgaria joined.

Yugoslavia was coerced into signing the Tripartite Pact on March 25, 1941 in Vienna. In fact, Yugoslavia had been in talks – under duress – with the fascist powers for months. Prince Paul had met Hitler at the beginning of March 1941, and Hitler hoped to neutralize the Balkans before he attacked the Soviet Union. He was also worried that Paul was a British stooge. Paul, on the other hand, ultimately agreed to the arrangement because he knew his country had no other reliable allies and he believed signing the pact might prolong Yugoslavia's autonomy. Prime Minister Dragiša Cvetković believed he had secured non-interference in Yugoslavia's affairs in return for the signing of the pact.[55]

As the 1930s constantly proved, assurances from Hitler and the Nazis were utterly worthless, and promises were abrogated through pretexts for military aggression. Yugoslavia's security may have seemed to have been reinforced by joining the Tripartite Pact, but within a matter of weeks, the country would be attacked by the Nazis and dismembered. On March 27, two days after the signing, Prince Paul was overthrown in a military coup with apparent British support. Demonstrators had come out onto the streets of Belgrade the previous day. The coup plotters, based in the Yugoslav Air Force, were also enraged by the signing of the Tripartite Pact and deposed Prince Paul and Prime Minister Cvetković. In their place the plotters installed the assassinated Alexander's son Peter, crowned as King Peter II. The new regime was pro-British and also supported by the Communist Party. At the same time, the coup was deemed as Serb-led and alarmed nationalities outside of the Serb heartlands.

There was also widespread anxiety that the coup would trigger war, and this is precisely what happened. When the new Yugoslav government refused to ratify the Tripartite Pact, it infuriated the Nazis, and Hitler issued the so-called "Directive 25." German forces attacked both Greece and Yugoslavia on April 6, 1941. The Luftwaffe bombed Belgrade for three days, and troops – in conjunction with Hungarian, Romanian and Italian forces – assaulted Yugoslavia from the

---

[55] Blanka Matkovich, *Croatia and Slovenia at the End and After the Second World War (1944-1945): Mass Crimes and Human Rights Violations Committed by the Communist Regime*, (Brown Walker Press, 2017), p. 30.

ground. The Yugoslav army was hopelessly outnumbered, poorly equipped and ill-prepared for aggression on this scale. It capitulated within a matter of days.[56]

The invading countries all wanted a piece of Yugoslavia's territory, and meanwhile, Ustaše leader Ante Pavelić declared an independent state of Croatia on April 10, 1941 while the fighting was still ongoing. The Yugoslav high command then surrendered unconditionally on April 18.

Under the aegis of Hitler, Yugoslavia was dismembered in a fashion to satisfy some of the claims of the Axis. Slovenia was divided and occupied by Germany and Italy, while Serbia was solely occupied by the Nazis. Bulgaria, under Boris III, was given Macedonia, and a puppet regime was installed in Montenegro. Italy claimed Kosovo, the region in the south of Serbia with a majority ethnic Albanian population, and Mussolini had already annexed Albania. Vojvodina, in the north of Serbia, was divided between Hungary and Germany. Finally, and most consequently, Pavelić's Independent Croatian State was recognized, including most of Bosnia and Herzegovina. The Nazis initially offered Maček the leadership of an independent Croatia, but he refused, instructing Croats to support the new state instead. Having spent most of the 1930s agitating for Croatian autonomy as well as organizing Ustaše terrorism, Pavelić had finally achieved his objective of a separate state. Although his Croatia was believed to be a fascist puppet of Italy and Germany, Pavelić would prove able to implement policies of his own accord.

Once the Nazis had pacified the Balkan region, they felt confident enough to invade the Soviet Union in the summer of 1941. In the former Yugoslavia, however, the new Croat regime wasted no time implementing its own version of fascism. Ante Pavelić took the position of *Poglavnik*, essentially a Croatian version of dictator, and set in motion a shocking set of ethno-nationalist policies. Pavelić met Hitler on several occasions during the war, including for the first time in Bavaria in June 1941, and it is believed that the German dictator gave his Croatian counterpart a lot of advice on how to run an effective fascist regime. Pavelić proved to be a faithful student of the Führer - he adorned himself with the usual fascist paraphernalia, including the military uniform, and also took to using the Nazi salute. The Zagreb regime also attempted to create a cult of personality around Pavelić.

The independent state of Croatia that existed between 1941 and 1945 was commonly known by the acronym NDH (*Nezavisna Država Hrvatska* in Serbo-Croat) and was essentially an Italian and German client. Nevertheless, the dictatorship of Ante Pavelić committed countless crimes against those within the territory he controlled.[57] It is estimated that as many as 700,000 people were killed in the NDH during this period, including ethnic Serbs and Jews, Roma, and Croats who opposed the regime. The methods used and the ideology which underpinned the crimes were chillingly similar to the Nazis. The Pavelić regime set up a secret service, the Ustaše

---

[56] The History Channel, '1941: Yugoslavia joins the Axis', (A&E Networks, 2009), https://www.history.com/this-day-in-history/yugoslavia-joins-the-axis, [accessed 21 August 2018]

[57] Ivo Goldstein, 'The Independent State of Croatia in 1941: On the Road to Catastrophe', *Totalitarian Movements and Political Religions*, 7:4, 2006, pp. 417-427.

Intelligence Service, which was charged with rooting out potential "enemies" of the state. A parliament was formed and met in 1942, but it rarely convened afterwards. Power within the NDH was concentrated in the hands of Pavelić and his Ustaše cronies.

The Nazi observers – representatives of one of history's most barbaric regimes – were themselves shocked by the extent of the violence in the NDH. The Nazis demanded that Pavelić implement anti-Semitic policies, which the NDH duly agreed to, but its primary focus was ethnically cleansing their state of Serbs. Pavelić was a racist and an ultra-nationalist who believed that Croatia needed to purge its Serbs, either through deportation, murder, or conversion to Catholicism.[58] Pavelić also installed lieutenants with predilections for extreme violence, such as head of the secret service, Eugen "Dido" Kvaternik, who was described as "bloodthirsty." The Slana death camp was quickly set up on the island of Pag, and then came the Jadovno camp. The majority of the prisoners were Serbs or Jews. The largest camp, however, would be built at Jasenovac, in the Croatian interior.[59] It was here, known as the "Auschwitz of the Balkans," that hundreds of thousands of people lost their lives. As historian Misha Glenny put it, it was not just the numbers but the ferocity of the killing in the NDH that put the Croatian Ustaše in its own vicious category. "Its (the NDH's) uniqueness lay in its brutality."[60] Jasenovac was described as a "slaughterhouse," where inmates could be bludgeoned to death with hammers, where humiliation and torture were endemic, and hygiene was so poor that diseases such as typhus were common.[61] Jasenovac was only the largest of many camps.

[58] Misha Glenny, *The Balkans 1804-2012: Nationalism, War and the Great Powers* (London: Granta, 2012), p. 498.
[59] David Owen, *Balkan Odyssey* (London: Indigo, 1996), p. 9.
[60] Misha Glenny, *The Balkans 1804-2012: Nationalism, War and the Great Powers* (London: Granta, 2012), p. 501.
[61] Ibid, p. 501.

A picture of Serbs being forced to convert to Catholicism

A picture of Ustaše members preparing to behead a Serb with a saw

Pavelić passed a decree in 1941 making all Jews, Serbs, and Roma "non-citizens" of the NDH. Croatia was therefore both active and complicit in the Holocaust. In 1930, around 856,000 Jewish people lived in the Balkans, and just 20 years later that number had fallen to less than 50,000 because of the genocide.[62] In the NDH, almost all Jews were killed during the war - a post-war Yugoslav report stated that out of the 30,000 Jews who lived in the NDH, only 1,500 survived. The Ustaše also targeted the Roma population, with about 30,000 being murdered in the NDH.

The status of Bosnian Muslims, ruled by the NDH from 1941-1945, was more ambiguous. The Ustaše state saw Bosnian Muslims as Croats of the Muslim faith, that is to say ethnically, if not

---

[62] Mark Mazower, *The Balkans: From the End of Byzantium to the Present Day* (London: Phoenix, 2001), p. 125.

religiously, homogeneous. Some Bosnian Muslims collaborated with the Croats in their campaign of ethnic cleansing, while some were victims themselves of NDH state violence.[63] Others, however, resisted the Ustaše and participated in the Partisan movement. Grotesque violence and ethnic cleansing also took place in the occupied zones of Serbia, Slovenia, and others.

By the summer of 1944, the Axis powers were having serious difficulties in the war. The United States and its allies had successfully landed in France and were rapidly driving back German forces there. The Soviets had also started to overrun the Nazis and were making quick progress as they pushed west. Other forces, also led by the United States, were driving back the fascists from the Mediterranean, and Italy had already capitulated. The existence of the NDH was now in the balance, and Zagreb was becoming wary of its fate should the Axis be defeated. Croatia was in jeopardy of occupation by either the democratic Allies or the communist Soviets, and it was understood that neither would be friendly towards the fascist ethno-nationalism of the Pavelić regime.

As a result of this growing uncertainty, the Foreign Minister, Mladen Lorković, and the Minister for War, Ante Vokić, attempted to overthrow Pavelić in a coup in August 1944. The attempt failed and the two men were executed. It was not until May 1945 that the NDH was finally toppled, with its leadership, including the *Poglavnik*, fleeing into exile. Ante Pavelić would spend the rest of his life on the run, eventually taking refuge in Franco's Spain, where he died in 1959.

Resistance

"The peoples of Yugoslavia do not want Fascism. They do not want a totalitarian regime, they do not want to become slaves of the German and Italian financial oligarchy as they never wanted to become reconciled to the semi-colonial dependence imposed on them by the so-called Western democracies after the first imperialist war." - Tito

Over the course of 1940, Tito swiftly expanded Communist Party of Yugoslavia membership, taking it from 1,500 to 8,000 members. Though still officially illegal, the CPY did achieve some measure of respectability when the older, failing, legal parties applied to it for help and advice. A communique authored by the CPY openly declared its intention to found a communist republic created from a broad-based revolution: "We communists consider that in this final hour it is essential to unite all those forces which are ready to struggle [...] however, we communists further consider that such militant unity will only really bring results when it is achieved not only between leaders but from below, among the depths of the working masses." (Swain, 2011, 29).

Tito sensed that the Germans might eventually invade Yugoslavia, anticipating this event as an

---

[63] David Owen, *Balkan Odyssey* (London: Indigo, 1996), p. 8.

opportunity. He planned for strong communist partisan forces to retreat to the mountains, while leaving agents behind in the towns. When the Germans eventually weakened, he thought, the partisans could sweep out of their montane fastnesses and conquer Yugoslavia in the name of Leninist revolution.

In fact, Tito had scarcely laid his plans before Hitler's panzer divisions roared over the Yugoslavian border. Ostensibly assisting the Croatians in their bid for independence, the Wehrmacht invaded on April 6th, 1941. With typical German speed, the 2nd and 12th Armies crashed through the Yugoslavian defenses, seizing the capital Belgrade by April 13th. The Royal Yugoslav Army surrendered on April 17th, ending official resistance.

In the wake of the Nazi conquest, the old divisions the monarchy attempted to paper over burst out afresh, perhaps strengthened and exaggerated by their brief suppression. The Croatians established the Independent State of Croatia, a curious mix of puppet state and independent ally on the side of the Germans. Intense partisan warfare soon began, launched by the Ustashe, an alliance of Catholic Croatians and Bosniak Muslims determined to drive out or eradicate the Serbs. Even the Germans found themselves somewhat taken aback at the extent of the massacres and violence committed by the Ustashe, with Edmund Glaise-Horstenau reporting that "according to reliable reports from countless German military and civilian observers during the last few weeks, in country and town, the Ustasha have gone raging mad." (West, 1994, 98).

Glaise-Horstenau initially attempted to protect the Serbs to some extent, but with only six battalions of Wehrmacht at his disposal, he could but stop just a small fraction of the violence. This, in turn, kindled an answering aggression in the Serbs, a pugnacious, defiant people throughout all of their history. Soon the Serbian Chetniks opposed the Ustashe, while collaborating to a considerable degree with the Axis forces in many areas. Ante Pavelic, head of the new Croatian state, assured Glaise-Horstenau repeatedly that he would rein in the Ustashe but never did so.

Pavelic and Hitler

Tito proved reluctant to seize the opportunity to become leader of the communist Partisan movement. He had married Herta Haas, his second wife, and did not wish to leave her and his new son. However, by May, events forced him to flee to Belgrade, where the communist leadership had already gone. Tito issued several proclamations, including an upbeat revolutionary document vowing that Yugoslavia would rise and throw off the occupier's yoke in a communist revolution. The killings by the Ustashe, otherwise known as the Black Legion, won him many Serbian recruits, as did oppressive Germanic rule. The various factions quickly mushroomed into armies; by the end of 1941, the Partisans already numbered 80,000 men and women, while the Chetniks fielded 20,000 and the Ustashe 16,000 supplemented by a powerful "Home Guard" of 85,000. All sides would eventually organize their forces into divisions as their numbers continued expanding.

Tito received the post of Commander-in-Chief of the National Liberation Army of Yugoslavia on June 27th, 1941, by decree of the Politboro of the Central Committee of the CPY. Wielding his new authority, Tito began operations almost immediately in Serbia proper. A region of forested hills and tough, fierce people, Serbia seemed an excellent starting point for establishing a Partisan base area. As Tito explained, "While looking over the configuration of the terrains of Serbia, I saw that western Serbia was most suitable for us, for the orientation of our fighting units, for the organisation of our partisan units and for the creation of a certain free territory […]

at the beginning we did not believe that we would create a large free territory so soon." (Swain, 2011, 35).

In fact, thanks to large numbers of Wehrmacht troops being withdrawn for participation in Operation Barbarossa, the invasion of the Soviet Union, Tito's initial plan experienced unexpected success. In August and September of 1941, the Partisans managed to seize most of Serbia, enabling Tito to relocate his headquarters to Uzice. A separate July uprising in Montenegro by the region's inhabitants, who lived up to the death-defying reputation their people had won over the centuries, ousted the Italians from much of Montenegro.

The Partisans' success in resisting the Germans and other factions came both from the intense fighting spirit and courage of all the Yugoslav ethnicities and their large stocks of weapons. Sporting and hunting rifles abounded in prewar Yugoslavia, enabling the partisans of all stripes to attack paramilitary and military posts, thereby obtaining further large caches of weapons in the process. Deserting Yugoslav army soldiers also supplied rifles, pistols, hand grenades, machine guns, and ammunition.

On September 19th, Tito met with Chetnik leader Dragoljub Mihailovic, known to his men as "Uncle Draza," a bearded, bespectacled man who would soon become Tito's bitter enemy. The two leaders formed a temporary alliance for the purpose of expanding the "free territory" already won. Tito wanted to go vigorously on the offensive, while Mihailovic urged a more cautious approach to avoid reprisals.

Mihailovic

Galled by the remarkable successes of the Partisans and resistance by numerous small bands of armed men loosely affiliated or unaffiliated with the major movements, the Germans launched the First Anti-Partisan Offensive on September 20th. The Chetniks attacked the Partisans at the same time as they fought the Germans, despite attempts by Tito and Mihailovic to negotiate a truce. The Serbians felt deep and not entirely unwarranted alarm by the fact that the Partisans enforced a monopoly of communist government in Western Serbia, suppressing other parties despite their strong support.

Two German divisions, strengthened by elements of four more and bolstered by two volunteer Serbian units, eventually threw the Partisans and Chetniks out of western Serbia, recapturing Uzice in the process. Tito himself barely escaped, leaving his headquarters, submachine gun in hand, just 20 minutes before German *Landsers* reached it. Remarking on this event, Tito admitted that "we did not think that the Germans would go through the liberated territory like a knife through butter, we expected steady pressure and that we would be able to hold on for a long time, that we would get more organised and produce more arms." (Swain, 2011, 41).

Tito offered his resignation to the Politboro in case they wanted to hold him responsible for the disaster, but he found himself left in command nevertheless. Mihailovic continued fighting the Germans also, though he observed that Tito's open resistance had indeed triggered several reprisal massacres by the Germans.

During 1942 and 1943, a seesaw battle moved back and forth across the landscape of Yugoslavia, as first the Germans and then the Partisans gained the upper hand. The gleeful ferocity of the Partisans often matched or exceeded that of their opponents, and the British intelligence officers attached to the Yugoslavian forces often found themselves stunned by the bloodthirsty relentlessness and outright cruelty of both their allies and foes. The intense resistance in Yugoslavia troubled the Axis leaders, Mussolini in particular. At the very end 1941, the Duce wrote to the Fuhrer, "Balkans. It is necessary to eliminate all the hotbeds of insurrection before spring. They might cause the broadening of the war in the Balkans. We should pacify Bosnia first, then Serbia and Montenegro. It is necessary for our armed forces to collaborate according to a common plan, in order to avoid a loss of energy and to reach the desired results with the least amount of men and material." (Dedijer, 1953, 184),

Hitler accepted this proposal, and the anti-partisan actions in Yugoslavia developed almost precisely as Mussolini laid out. The Second Anti-Partisan Offensive began in January 1942 and continued through February, evicting the Partisans from Eastern Serbia. The follow-up operation, the Third Anti-Partisan Offensive, aimed not only at Serbia but also at Bosnia, Herzegovina, and Montenegro. During the Third Partisan Offensive, the Germans, Italians, Ustashe, and those Chetniks who now openly cooperated with the invaders in anti-Partisan operations pushed forward slowly against heavy resistance in March 1942. The protracted offensive continued throughout April and into early May.

On May 1st, Tito held the Partisan Olympics at Foca. With the Commander-in-Chief as a spectator, teams from the Supreme HQ, First Proletarian Brigade, and assorted other units contended at volleyball, soccer, and field and track. At this point, the leading Italian units continued their advance just 7 miles distant. After the Olympics, Tito withdrew his five Proletarian Brigades into the mountains between Bosnia and Montenegro, eluding an Axis encirclement attempt. At one point, Tito came across a small abandoned mill and, overtaken by his old obsession, worked for 30 minutes on the mill machinery. Once the mill started working again, Tito and his men moved on.

From there, the Proletarian Brigades and other Partisan units launched a counteroffensive in Eastern Bosnia. Tito liberated the regional capital Bihac, along with 10 other towns, with 30,000 Partisans installed as a garrison force. Though the Partisans endured numerous hardships campaigning in the rough terrain and wild countryside, they maintained a high esprit de corps, as one account suggests: "After two days of battle, we were tired, dirty and hungry. Passing through a town, the people there ran out onto the streets to wave at and greet us. The battalion commander told one soldier with a strong voice to lead the troops in a song. They sang with him, loudly and clearly. We raised our heads, our exhaustion disappeared and each step became stronger and more resolute. The people watched us and admired us. They said, "There goes the people's army, the Proletarians."" (Vuksic, 2003, 31).

The Germans called this liberated area "Tito's Territory," clearly recognizing the figurehead and mastermind behind the massively successful Partisan movement. Tito, though a communist and therefore officially an atheist, ordered his men to restore the Serbian churches dismantled or decommissioned by the Ustashe. This won him immense popularity among the masses of ordinary Serbs, who provided him with hundreds of thousands of fearlessly aggressive infantry. By late 1942, Tito's Partisans mustered so many men and women that a larger unit – the Corps, consisting of 9 divisions – appeared in the organizational table of the growing army. The Partisans had almost reached the organization and professionalism of a regular army, though they proved just as apt to commit massacres as the Ustashe.

In the beginning of 1943, the Germans and Italians under General Alexander von Leer launched the Fourth Anti-Partisan Offensive, also known as Operation White (*Fall Weiss*). 90,000 men supported by 12 air squadrons participated in the offensive. These included the 7th SS Volunteer Mountain Division *Prinz Eugen* under SS-Gruppenfuhrer Artur Gustav Phleps, and the 369th (Croatian) Infantry Division, known as the "Devil's Division" (Teufels-Division), among others. Marking the unusual nature of the Yugoslavian war, the Chetniks fought alongside the Italians – as allies, rather than servants or collaborators – yet retained a deadly enmity with the Germans. While the Chetniks attacked the communist Partisans, they remained prepared to attack the Germans also, while the German High Command ordered their troops to wipe out the Chetniks if they came in contact with them.

This bizarre mix of enmity and alliance did not flow in only one direction. Tito opened negotiations with the Germans for a time in March, and during that interval, he issued an order to his troops: "On your way, do not fight Germans […] Your most important task at this moment is to annihilate the Chetniks of Draza Mihailovic and to destroy their command apparatus which represents the greatest danger to the development of the National Liberation Struggle."(Roberts, 1987, 102).

With his characteristic audacity and initiative, Tito turned the Fourth Anti-Partisan Offensive into a springboard for a Partisan offensive into Montenegro. The Partisans seized most of Montenegro and smashed the Chetniks as a military force, after which the Germans mopped up their remnants and nearly managed to capture or kill Mihailovic.

1943 witnessed two more offensives against Tito's forces. The Fifth Anti-Partisan Offensive struck at Tito's new "free territories" in Montenegro, using 117,000 men supported by over 300 combat aircraft. Heavy fighting continued for months, during which the Germans killed 7,543 Partisan combatants, suffering 913 KIA and 2,132 MIA (probably KIA, given the universal tendency to take no prisoners). This offensive, Operation Black, nevertheless failed, leaving the Partisans in control of Montenegro.

Tito and Ivan Ribar in 1943

The Sixth Offensive occurred in the east towards the end of the year, aiming at Bosnia. Consisting of Operation Kugelblitz and Operation Schneesturm (Ball Lightning and Snowstorm), the offensive inflicted heavy losses on the Partisans but failed to break up the structure of their units, thus proving largely futile.

During the harsh fighting in Yugoslavia, Tito developed his own set of military rules, designed to amplify the strengths of his irregular Partisan forces. He always ordered the utmost efforts to be given to care for the wounded. In the event of an enemy offensive, safe evacuation of the wounded took top priority, and, in fact, formed the focus of several major battles during the Fourth and Fifth Offensives. Tito believed this increased the morale of his men, and considering the daring and courage often showed by his Partisans, reality seemingly bore out the concept's validity.

Tito also worked hard to inculcate his soldiers with the idea that being surrounded did not mean their doom. Instead, the Partisans received training to pick a single spot in encircling troops and throw their full weight against it vigorously. This almost always permitted a successful breakout even against superior numbers.

Two other precepts of "Tito-style warfare" included the necessity for officers to undergo the same risks as ordinary soldiers, thus preventing resentment, and rear area spoiling attacks during enemy advances. Any major forward thrust by German, Italian, or Ustashe forces triggered deployment of numerous Partisan raiding parties, who infiltrated the rear of the advancing force. These men and women then did their best to disrupt hostile communications to the utmost, making the advance more difficult and less coordinated.

With the Allies in Italy, just across the Adriatic, and an invasion of Normandy looming (though the extensive British deception plan made the Germans believe Calais the main target), the Germans made a desperate but well-planned effort to eliminate the guiding spirit of the Partisans – Tito himself – in 1944. The year opened with Tito executing another of his key maneuvers – when pushed out of one area by an Axis offensive, immediately and simultaneously launching an offensive into a fresh area to gain new territory. As he described this method, "[W]e must not let the enemy force us by clever tactics onto the defensive. We must make up for the loss of one area by the conquest of a larger and more important area." (Greentree, 2012, 13-14).

Tito and the Partisan Supreme Command in May 1944

This time, however, the Germans clearly identified Tito's strategy. The Abwehr deployed 10 FAT (Frontaufklärungstruppe) intelligence teams, who developed a network of local agents to pin down Tito's location. Finally, the Germans deployed an elite unit of Brandenburger Commandos known as the Benesch Special Unit to track the elusive Partisan Commander-in-Chief down. Disguising themselves as farmers and partisans, these men infiltrated the region where intelligence suggested Tito might be found, near the town of Drvar in a valley of the Dinaric Alps. These daring men, knowing certain death awaited them if captured out of uniform, infiltrated among the equally daring Partisans.

To the particular alarm of Tito's lieutenants, they uncovered and captured a German agent within the Partisan leader's headquarters staff in March 1944. Worse, from their viewpoint, the German managed to escape from the cell where he awaited execution and vanished into the countryside. Tito began using one alpine cave as his HQ and sleeping in another to make his location harder to pin down.

Eventually, the Germans decided to send in a unique unit to kill Tito, the 500th SS Parachute Battalion. Formed mainly of SS men who had been sentenced to a special detention camp for minor disciplinary infractions, the Battalion also included a range of volunteers. These men received training in parachute and glider operations, and soon numbered 1,140, organized into 5 companies. The operation, dubbed Operation Rösselsprung or Knight's Move (a chess term), involved dropping the 500th SS Parachute Battalion directly in the valley near Drvar, following a preparatory Stuka dive-bombing attack. Simultaneously, five motorized columns would converge on the suspected location of Tito's headquarters. Several dozen DFS 230 gliders would provide the means for the 500th's airborne assault.

Tito should have been at Bastasi when the attack came on May 25th, 1944, but he had remained at Drvar due to the fact he celebrated his birthday on that date (rather than the actual date of May 7th). Tito's cave headquarters represented a well-appointed lodging, as a description underlines: "In a natural cleft in the rock three flights of wooden steps led to [...] a natural cave, inside which rooms had been constructed with a veranda in front commanding a fine view across the valley. Great wooden beams supported the construction and inside in Tito's office the walls were lined, and the windows curtained with parachute silk, while a huge British military map of Yugoslavia covered a wall behind his desk." (Greentree, 2012, 30).

Just after sunrise on May 25th, 14 Stuka dive-bombers and a squadron of Italian light bombers attacked suspected Partisan positions in and around Drvar. Immediately after the bombing, a wave of paratroopers from the 500th SS Parachute Battalion landed, followed by the main force in gliders. The Germans landed in a wide arc around Drvar, often very close to their objectives, while more landed on the heights above the town to seal off escape into the forested mountains. A ferocious firefight erupted at the Communist Party Central Committee headquarters, which the Germans mistook for a communications center. The SS men cleared the building after a lethal gun-battle.

The Germans, working efficiently, cleared Drvar of resistance by 9 AM, taking a high number of prisoners. At this point, three captured CV-35 tanks – light Italian designs – counterattacked the Germans with their machine guns. The Germans had no antitank weapons available to counter these small vehicles, which pinned them down for several minutes. SS Oberscharführer Hummel ran to one of the tanks and blocked its vision slit with his camouflage smock. However, a 16-year-old female Partisan, Mika Bosnic, rushed to the tank, and, before the Germans shot her, pulled the smock clear. The tanks soon retreated, presumably having exhausted their machine gun ammunition.

One of the prisoners almost immediately revealed the location of Tito's cave, pointing reflexively to its location when a German showed him the Partisan leader's photograph. Tito soon observed German soldiers closing on the cave across the valley floor. SS machine gun teams set up heavy machine guns, sited to prevent anyone from leaving the cave mouth alive.

Tito, along with the 12 men and 8 women in the cave with him, escaped through the floor. Cutting through the floorboards, they lowered a rope ladder into the stream flowing under part of the HQ, Thick vegetation hid the streambed from observation, and the partisans had earlier placed a rope ladder up the cleft of the falling stream to the plateau above. Tito, his followers, and his Alsatian dog Tiger climbed up to safety. As Tito put it, "I left with the help of my escort and my dog, Tiger. After we climbed for a while, I had to take a rest. Tiger came to me. He started to whine. I grabbed him by the snout to keep him quiet. There were times that I thought we would have to shoot him with a pistol, because he would betray us, but I couldn't bring myself to do it." (Greentree, 2012, 52-53).

With Tito clear, the Partisans mounted increasingly powerful counterattacks against the 500th SS Parachute Battalion, forcing it back into a defensive perimeter. The Germans held out overnight despite constant heavy attacks, with the Partisans drawing off at morning when Luftwaffe air support arrived. Later on May 26th, the German motorized forces arrived, including the feared 7th SS Division "Prinz Eugen." After some additional fighting, the Partisans retreated, as a German officer recounted: "We stormed up the hill and in a single rush, firing from the hip and lobbing hand grenades, we crushed the enemy. The entire regiment […] pursued the enemy as he   fled to the north. The latter offered no resistance, because their objective of enabling Tito to escape had been achieved. Tito got away, though […] he had to leave his brand new Marshal's uniform behind." (Kurowski, 2005, 269).

After his escape, Tito allowed the Allies to evacuate him, first by air and then by sea, to the island of Vis in the Adriatic. There he set up his headquarters in another cave. The Germans soon located him there, but the island's defenses proved so formidable that they made no further attempts on the Partisan leader there.

At this moment, politics entered the picture amid the continuing military operations. British Prime Minister Winston Churchill sent Ivan Subasic to Vis, compelling Tito, using the lever of British aid, to nominally accept the legitimacy of King Petar, currently in exile in England. Tito felt rather displeased at this, preferring not to have any dealings with the monarchy due to his communist leanings. Nonetheless, Tito traveled to confer with Winston Churchill in Naples on August 12th. At the meeting, the Partisan leader promised to allow a multi-party democracy in Yugoslavia, essentially promising the Englishman whatever he wanted as long as Allied support for the Yugoslavian Partisans continued.

Tito and Churchill in Italy in 1944

On the night of September 18th to 19th, 1944, Tito slipped off Vis on a journey to Moscow, which he did not warn the British about. In Moscow, he met with Stalin, and Tito took a surprisingly independent tone in his conference with the Soviet strongman, essentially stating that if the Soviets did not assist him, they should at least stand out of his way. Hearing Tito still complaining about King Petar, Stalin offered some avuncular counsel: "You don't have to return him forever. Only for a while, then slip a knife into his back at the opportune moment." (Banac, 1988, 14).

Stalin and Tito agreed that the Soviets would take Belgrade and leave the rest of Yugoslavia's liberation to the Partisans, which is exactly what happened. Except for a Soviet incursion as far as Belgrade, the now gigantic, 800,000-strong Partisan army swept forward on a last offensive in late 1944 and into 1945. Carrying all resistance before them, the Yugoslavian forces smashed the last resistance by May 15th, 1945, a week after V-E Day marked Germany's unconditional surrender. Tito would say of the war, "Our sacrifices are terrible. I can safely say that there is no other part of the world which has been devastated on a vaster scale than Yugoslavia. Every tenth Yugoslav has perished in this struggle in which we were forced to wrest armaments from our enemies, to freeze without clothing, and to die without medication. Nevertheless our optimism and faith have proved justified. The greatest gain of this conflict between democracy and fascism lies in the fact that it has drawn together everything that was good in humanity. The unity of the United States, the Soviet Union and Great Britain is the best guarantee to the peoples of the world that Nazi horrors will never again be repeated."

A celebration held for Tito near the end of the war

World War II in Czechoslovakia

The Allies had abandoned Czechoslovakia in its hour of need, and that pattern repeated itself until the German invasion of Poland in 1939. Finally drawing a line in the sand, Britain and France declared war on Germany, starting the most destructive war the world has ever known.

Although the area was not involved in heavy fighting, the Czechs and Slovaks suffered extreme brutality during the war, and the Czechs would be involved in the war's most notorious assassination.

The British Special Operations Executive, or SOE, and the Czechoslovakian government in exile under President Beneš cooperated in creating a plan to kill Heydrich. The operation received the somewhat bizarre codename "Operation Anthropoid" and originated with the Czech exiles. The British government placed increasing pressure on these displaced officials to come up with a plan bolstering Czech resistance to Nazi occupation. Accordingly, in September 1941, the Czechs picked Heydrich as an assassination target, and the SOE assisted preparations.

As if that poor track record wasn't enough cause for concern, the Czechs had divided support for the plan amongst themselves; in fact, powerful political disagreements amongst themselves characterized the Czechs during Germany's occupation. One faction, standing for democracy, wanted to see Czechoslovakia as an independent nation in the manner of France or Britain, and while the United States fully supported this faction, the British offered tepid, unenthusiastic assistance due in large part to the fact that they had signed away just such a state in the 1938 Munich Agreement and had difficulty admitting their error. The other Czechoslovakian faction espoused radical communist beliefs, called for the overthrow of the Western democracies assisting them, and wished to see Czechoslovakia become an effective province of the Soviet Union.

Portrait of Palmer

The Czechs themselves remained dubious as to the value of armed resistance against the Nazis. Only the Third Reich's brutality provided some catalyst to resistance beyond the Czech norms of manipulating and passively resisting their conquerors. Nevertheless, many Czechs remained opposed to killing Heydrich outright, with good reason, as the event proved. Deciding to kill Heydrich from the safety of well-appointed quarters in England was a far different matter than facing the consequences of the assassination on the ground in Czechoslovakia, and as it happened, the Czech resistance, after helping to set up the Heydrich assassination scheme, made an 11th hour attempt to persuade the government in exile to abandon it. According to one historian, on May 12th, 1942, just 15 days prior to the assassination, "several senior members of the Czech underground sent a radio message toLondon urging President Beneš to cancel the assassination, citing three major reasons: that thousands of hostages in German hands would be executed, that the Nazis would commence unprecedented massacres, and that the last remnants of the underground resistance would be wiped out."

These fears proved to be eerily accurate, as every single one of them became a reality during the days following the attack on Reinhard Heydrich. By then, however, President Beneš thought the plot was too far advanced to abandon, and the British remained sanguine that increased Czech resistance, or even a general uprising, would ensue once the Gestapo general died and demonstrated the human vulnerability of the Nazis.

Though the matter is disputed among historians, it is possible that Beneš and his fellow Czech government exiles acted in response to a considerably more sinister motivation themselves. Though Heydrich contemptuously referred to his charges, in private, as "Czech garbage," and he privately claimed that only a minority of them presented suitable characteristics to make proper German citizens, his public actions paradoxically tended to make him more popular as time passed. Heydrich's initially bloody introductory period ended rather quickly, and while he continued to harry and deport Jews, the average Czech on the street began to profit from Heydrich's rule over Czechoslovakia. Whether Heydrich possessed the intelligence, lacking in so many other prominent Nazis, to realize that conquered peoples might be induced to support the Third Reich if the Germans offered benefits instead of oppression and murder, or whether Czechoslovakia simply had such high industrial value that the Nazis made an exception to their usual method of tormenting and impoverishing their foreign subjects, the "Blond Beast's" actions alarmed Beneš in a different manner, according to some historians. One British historian provides a concise summary of President Eduard Beneš' potential motivation for ordering Heydrich's assassination even in the teeth of heartfelt protests from his own nation's homegrown resistance movement. These represent serious charges which, if true, place Beneš in the light of a ruthless man willing to deliberately trigger the murder of thousands of men, women, and children in his nation simply to retain his political influence among the survivors. If this assessment is accurate, then Beneš emerges on the page of history as an unusual type of war criminal, deliberately provoking genocidal acts against his own nation and people in order to profit from their misery.

That said, in the absence of any documentary proof pointing precisely to Beneš' thoughts on the subject, proving the government in exile's culpability remains difficult. Nevertheless, the suspicion, unlike many conspiracy theories, is not implausible, given the thorough, detailed warnings of Nazi retribution Beneš received and the fact that he chose to ignore them entirely. These strong hints of malevolent intent cast doubts on the assassination of Reinhard Heydrich as an act of heroic tyrannicide and recast it more strongly as a cruelly selfish decision by exiled politicians determined to retain their own influence and luxurious lifestyle regardless of the human cost.

The SOE and Czech exiles conducted a supporting operation in early October 1941 entitled Operation Percentage, which involved dropping radios and their operators into Czechoslovakia to facilitate communications between the Czech resistance and Britain. However, the Gestapo located one of the main transmitters on the first night, seizing and torturing the operators to learn more details of what was underway. The Germans made use of what was, for their era, a high-tech solution; radio detecting vehicles prowled the streets of Czech cities, and once an illegal transmitter was detected, Gestapo agents closed in using small, belt-mounted Kapsch radio locators. This early man-portable tracking technology proved extremely effective, enabling a wave of arrests that alarmed both the British and the Czech government in exile.

Driven by fear that the Nazis would wipe out the resistance before their agents arrived to kill Heydrich, the SOE accelerated the timetable vastly. As the Czechs conducted reconnaissance, the local resistance leader, Bartos, an extremely sick man, anticipated the horrific consequences of the assassination and tried to dissuade the men from moving forward with Operation Anthropoid. The assassins initially kept their mission secret, but Bartos pieced the information together and confronted the men in April, just a month before the assassination took place. He begged them to reconsider in light of the massacres the Nazis would carry out to avenge Heydrich's death. The assassins, Gabcik and Kubis, met these demands with stony refusal and eventually stormed out in a rage.

While this squabbling went on, the Gestapo managed to intercept and translate part of the Czech transmission, warning them that the Czechs planned some kind of commando operation in the near future. One unknown factor is whether the British SOE would have called off the operation had they known the resistance's objections and the probability of compromised communications. However, Beneš and his lieutenants did not inform the English of the communication or the doubts it contained, and SOE itself did not learn of the dispute until after the end of the war.

Either way, the Gestapo formed a clear picture of rising Czech "terrorism," and Himmler himself grew alarmed enough to visit Prague on May 1st, slightly more than three weeks before Heydrich's assassination. The Gestapo noted large numbers of commandos and saboteurs, as well as the capture of explosives, booby-trapped telephones which exploded when a person lifted the receiver, and so on. Himmler asked Heydrich to improve the security situation in the light of these developments, but Heydrich still refused to use a personal escort.

The Anthropoid assassins received a final impetus to act from Heydrich's schedule; when Hitler called for the Gestapo general to return to Berlin on May 27th, 1942, the men knew this might be their last opportunity. Accordingly, they chose a killing ground suited to their purposes. Along the road from his castle to Prague, Heydrich drove down a hill to the Troja bridge in the Holešovice suburb, and at the bottom of the hill, the road went around an extreme hairpin turn, forcing all cars to slow to a crawl for several seconds to avoid skidding off the road. Moreover, a tram stop nearby provided the men with an excuse to loiter in the area without drawing unwanted attention, and no police stations or Gestapo barracks stood nearby. The plan was to kill Heydrich, either with a burst of fire from a Sten gun or with a hand grenade, then escape to nearby safe houses using bicycles.

The preparations and scouting had required so much time that the two men only prepared to carry out their orders on May 27th just a few hours before Heydrich left Prague by airplane for his meeting with Hitler in Germany, where he might possibly be given a reassignment to a different location. Operation Anthropoid would occur almost literally at the 11th hour.

Reinhard Heydrich and the men planning to kill him both woke up to a beautiful morning on May 27, 1942. This was to be Heydrich's last day in Czechoslovakia for some time at least, and, apparently savoring a moment of pleasurable sentimentality, the Blonde Beast abandoned his usual clockwork routine and driven punctuality. Instead, after rising at the Lower Castle in Panenské Břežany, he ate a leisurely breakfast, which only ended at around 9:00 in the morning.

Heydrich, his mind no doubt far removed from the scenes of horror for which he bore considerable responsibility, enjoyed an hour relaxing with his family before he finally climbed into his black Mercedes touring car. The car's open top allowed ample fresh air and sunlight, but it also exposed the occupants to bullets, grenades, and even such simple weapons as thrown rocks or roofing tiles. Only two men sat in the car: Heydrich, in the back seat, and his driver, Oberscharfuhrer (Staff Sergeant) Johannes Klein, in the driver's seat.

In contrast to their reprehensibly sloppy behavior during the five months leading up to this moment, Gabcik and Kubis acted methodically on the morning of the assassination attempt, and Josef Valcik accompanied them as a spotter. The men carried their weapons inside a pair of briefcases.

The men took a tram to the suburb where they had left their bicycles, retrieved them, and pedaled onward to Liben, where they took up their positions at the hairpin curve chosen as the ambush site. Valcik moved up the hill to a prearranged observation point, where he waited with his shaving mirror in his pocket to flash a signal to his comrades when he spotted the sleek black Mercedes convertible approaching.

Gabcik assembled his Sten gun underneath a light-colored raincoat he had brought for this purpose, then lurked as unobtrusively as possible near the tram stop as if he was waiting for one. Kubis, with his two grenades, stood on the opposite side of the street in the shade of a clump of trees, again trying to avoid drawing attention.

Finally, at 10:20 a.m. (some accounts say 10:32 or 10:35), Valcik spotted the black Mercedes 320-C convertible gliding down the street. A tram approached the hairpin turn from the opposite direction, but the assassins had already agreed that civilian casualties would be acceptable if necessary to carry out Heydrich's killing. Valcik pulled the shaving mirror from his pocket and flashed it in the sun in the direction of his comrades near the hairpin turn, and the two men saw the brilliant flash of sunlight off Valcik's mirror and prepared themselves for the moment of action.

As the Mercedes 320-C slowed to a walking pace to round the hairpin curve, Gabcik ran out onto the sidewalk, throwing aside the raincoat to level his Sten gun at the car and its two Nazi occupants. The Sten gun, a cheap 9mm submachine gun with a folding stock, featured a stamped metal build and a 32 round magazine. The British, whose long-standing gun control had thoroughly disarmed their populace and necessitated the importation of 5,000 donated firearms from the United States at the start of the war to provide the home guard with some kind of weaponry, had produced the Sten gun in vast numbers in an effort to arm their own forces and those of anti-Nazi insurgents throughout Europe.

The simple weapon, which fired pistol ammunition, seldom hit anything beyond 100 yards, but Gabcik stood just a few feet from his targets as he raised the Sten gun and squeezed the trigger. At this juncture, he learned another characteristic of the Sten: its tendency to stop working unless given constant maintenance to avoid a host of other problems and circumstances. Rather than a rattling burst of bullets shredding the two Nazis in front of him, the Czech heard only silence as he yanked frantically on the trigger. His Sten gun, brought so painstakingly to this point, was as useless as a toy.

At this moment, Heydrich and Klein each made a mistake that resulted in the Gestapo chief's death. Heydrich ordered his driver to stop, and Klein obeyed. Rather than accelerating out of the ambush, the aggressive Heydrich decided to capture or kill Gabcik, whom he incorrectly assumed was acting alone. Meanwhile, Kubis grabbed one of the anti-tank grenades out of his worn briefcase and sprinted out of the trees. The two Nazis, their attention focused on Gabcik, who still struggled futilely with his Sten gun a few feet away, would fail to notice the second attacker until it was too late.

Kubis acted decisively but clumsily. One historian explained, "He misjudged his throw. Instead of landing inside the Mercedes, it exploded against the rear wheel, throwing shrapnel back into Kubiš' face and shattering the windows of the tram which had stopped on the opposite side of the road. There were screams as the passengers were hit by shards of flying glass and metal. The car lurched violently and came to rest in the gutter, pouring smoke. Two SS jackets which had been folded on the back seat were whirled upwards by the blast and draped themselves over the trolley wire."

Pictures of the damaged car and tram

Despite the poor toss, Heydrich had suffered severe injuries in the blast, the worst being a large piece of shrapnel which ripped through his back and deep into his spleen. However, the Gestapo chief was so full of adrenaline that he didn't feel his injuries, and thinking he was unharmed, he jumped out of the car and staggered towards Gabcik, trying to get a clear shot with his 7.65mm pistol. Gabcik stood for several moments, staring stupefied at the tall, blond man in the black uniform stumbling towards him through the smoke and dust. Then, despite the shock of the explosion, the Czech made a stumbling run uphill. As he fled, the crack of pistol shots sounded behind him, and bullets whined past him. Desperately, he jumped behind a telephone pole and fired back at his black-garbed pursuer. Heydrich moved behind the damaged tram and returned fire, hoping to cripple or kill Gabcik.

Gabcik began to despair, knowing that SS men would arrive on the scene very soon. However, as the gunfight continued, Heydrich suddenly dropped to the ground; the pain from his wound suddenly struck him, and he writhed in agony for several moments. Gabcik, terrified, did not return to finish his target off but fled uphill, diving through the open door of a butcher shop up the road.

Despite the severity of his injuries, the mortally wounded Heydrich did not die shortly after the grenade seriously injured him. In fact, he lived for more than a week, dying eight days later on June 3rd at precisely the moment his relieved doctors believed he was about to make a full recovery. Heydrich received a state funeral from the Third Reich in a gigantic Berlin ceremony. After lying in state for two days in the courtyard of Prague Castle, the Gestapo general's remains journeyed by aircraft to the Reich's capital, where he was laid to rest amid solemn speeches by prominent Nazis (including Adolf Hitler himself) to the sound of the funeral march from the "Twilight of the Gods" by Richard Wagner.

A picture of Heydrich's funeral

Predictably, the Germans responded furiously to the brazen attack on a high Nazi official, which included launching an immediate manhunt for the perpetrators. While Reinhard Heydrich's troubles were, in a sense, over, those of Czechoslovakia were only just beginning.

Helmuth von Pannwitz, the chief of the Prague Gestapo's anti-sabotage branch, raised the alarm after he investigated a vague Czech police report of assassins wounding a German officer and found Heydrich being prepped for surgery at the Bulovka hospital. The other Nazis initially believed Pannwitz's report to be a practical joke, but his desperation eventually convinced them and a large detachment of heavily armed SS moved to the hospital to defend the "Reich Protector."

As news of the attack spread, ordinary Germans in the region grew enraged and began attacking Czechs, throwing bricks or firebombs into Czech stores and trying to kill Czechs they had lived alongside all their lives. The Gestapo and ordinary police protected the Czechs from this violence, which would lead to social disorder, but ultimately, the cruelty to be visited on the Czechoslovakian population would be officially organized, not a matter of vigilantism.

Hitler himself responded with a characteristic lack of restraint when he learned of Heydrich's wounding at 12:45 p.m. on May 27. According to one writer, "Infuriated, the Fuhrer ordered the arrest and execution of 10,000 Czech hostages. [...] German police collected all available evidence and concluded the attack must have been organized and prepared in England. Frank telephoned Hitler to confirm the British involvement and asked him to revoke the execution order, arguing that such unprecedented reprisals would be catastrophic for Czech morale." Though Hitler agreed to stop the immediate execution of 10,000 Czechs, he remained adamant that blood must be spilled in response to the attack. The Third Reich offered a reward of 10 million Czech koruna ("crowns") for information leading to the hiding place of the assassins, and at the same time, the highest members of the Nazi hierarchy discussed what response to the assassination attempt would be most appropriate. Propaganda minister Joseph Goebbels voiced fear that assassinations would multiply if they did not offer an overwhelming response: "It is imperative that we get hold of the assassins. Then a tribunal should be held to deal with them and their accomplices. The background of the attack is not yet clear. But it is revealing that London reported on the attack very early on. We must be clear that such an attack could set a precedent if we do not counter it with the most brutal of means."

   With these preliminary steps taken, the German commanders began their work in earnest. They mobilized 12,000 men, including men from the Gestapo, Wehrmacht, SS, Orpo, and the Czech police force, and began a massive sweep of Prague. The Germans searched over 36,000 buildings, yet, amazingly, discovered no clue as to the assassins' location, even though Gabcik, Kubis, and six other resistance personnel occupied a central position in the city of Prague the whole time. The men moved from one safe house to another for several days until they found their way to the Karel Boromejsky church at the city's heart. There, they hid themselves in the dim crypt beneath the white-walled stone building, already effectively buried and spending their days among the dead of centuries past. News reached them of Heydrich's death and the hideous vengeance extracted by the Germans, and while the first news cheered them, all of the men – and the two assassins, Gabcik and Kubis, in particular – felt a deep sense of guilt for the terror unleashed by the Nazis in response to their actions.

   Gabcik and Kubis eventually concocted a scheme which they hoped would put a stop to the Germans' program of revenge killing. The two men initially thought to go to a public park and shoot themselves there while wearing placards declaring their sole guilt in Heydrich's assassination. They then altered their plan to instead go to the office of Emanuel Moravec, a prominent Nazi collaborator, confess to the assassination of Heydrich, then kill Moravec also before taking cyanide pills. However, the other resistance men sharing their refuge talked them out of these steps, arguing – probably correctly – that the Nazis would continue their massacres regardless of the gesture.

   Eventually, Pannwitz acted as what might be called the voice of reason among the Nazis. He believed that the far-flung terror tended to silence those who knew something of the assassins out of fear that they and their families would be executed for not speaking up sooner. This measure prompted the breakthrough the Germans hoped for when an anonymous letter arrived at Gestapo headquarters, among 200 other letters, naming Gabcik and Kubis as the two men who killed Heydrich and pleading with the Nazis to stop killing people who had nothing to do with the assassination. A day later, the letter's writer, a Sergeant Curda, walked into Gestapo headquarters and gave himself up. Stammering in acute terror, he gave the Germans the names of those involved in the plot. A parachutist himself and a brave soldier earlier in the war, Curda appears to have simply grown sick of the slaughter and believed that Beneš' scheme to kill Heydrich was the act of a man detached from the real, actual horrors his decisions inflicted on the people of Czechoslovakia.

Curda did not know where the assassins were hiding, but he was able to betray the location of several safe houses. Nonetheless, even after the SS found and killed the assassins, the reprisals were far from over. In fact, the fates of Gabcik and Kubis are largely overlooked in comparison to the mention of Lidice, the most notorious target of Nazi vengeance. The Gestapo and SS began a program of ruthless murder in Czechoslovakia which eventually left some 5,000 Czechs dead, and Lidice, considered a hotbed of resistance by the Nazis, would be completely destroyed. As one writer explained, "On the day of Heydrich's state funeral [...] the village of Lidice, near Prague, was set on fire and entirely leveled by the SS for allegedly sheltering the parachute agents. Two hundred male inhabitants were shot on the spot, its female population sent to concentration camps, and the children given to German families for adoption. [...] In an act of spontaneous solidarity, several localities in the United States adopted its name."

Pictures of massacred victims at Lidice

A picture of Lidice in the wake of the Nazis' destruction of it

Out of the children given up for adoption, only 21 of the 102 survived. The other 81 were sent to Poland, crammed into a "gas van," and asphyxiated with exhaust fumes, a method so cruel that the SS and SD themselves eventually abandoned it due to the psychological shock caused by the sounds coming from inside the vans during the gassing process. The Germans exterminated another village on the day when the parachutists died in the church crypt, in revenge for the men's escape through suicide.

One of the Nazis' gas vans

Photographs still survive showing the ground littered with the corpses with Czech men executed by the Nazis during the revenge killings that followed. Guards drove bands of Jews out of their barracks in the concentration camps and gunned them down in reprisal for what the Nazis termed "a plot by the international Jewish conspiracy." Only with the coming of autumn did the killing abate, leaving a shocked and cowed Czechoslovakia in its wake.

The wheels of Hitler's ghoulish extermination scheme rolled on with well-oiled efficiency in the wake of Heydrich's death. Indeed, the Nazis accelerated the pace of human extirpation towards its logical limits following the assassination, in revenge for – and in honor of – their slain colleague. Just as Heydrich's death failed to impact the practical implementation of the Final Solution and other Nazi butchery, so it proved militarily insignificant. Heydrich's role was that of a secret police chief and mass murderer, and though he was recklessly brave in combat, Heydrich never commanded German armies, so his death made no military difference to the course of the war. The Third Reich's fighting machine remained the finest in the world at the time, though burdened by a factor ultimately proving to be its undoing: the incompetent, megalomaniac interference of Adolf Hitler in strategic planning.

The hope that the bold assassination would trigger greater resistance among the Czechs also backfired resoundingly on Operation Anthropoid's planners. Czechoslovakia, despite its relatively favored status in the Reich, resented the Nazi invasion, and "a non-communist resistance had existed from the beginning of the German occupation, and after almost complete destruction […] was reorganized in 1943 and 1944." (Skilling, 1960, 181). Heydrich's death, however, prompted such a violent retaliation from the Germans that it set back the resistance's timetable rather than advancing it. The Nazi terror cowed the Czechs for several years, leaving it to the ethnic Slovaks to stage an armed rebellion against the Nazis in autumn 1944. "[T]he Slovak people [...] carried through their own liberation before the arrival of the Red Army and, for approximately two months, governed themselves through the Slovak national council. […] In 1944, plans were laid for an uprising, and with the approval of Beneš, Lieutenant-Colonel Golian was appointed military commander. […] Open revolt spread throughout the area, partisan groups and Slovak army units taking part."

In short, Heydrich's death triggered such unbridled violence from the Germans that the ethnic Czechs remained largely supine for the rest of the occupation, and even the Slovaks only managed to arrange an uprising after years passed. This lack of active resistance during 1942, 1943, and much of 1944 cemented Czechoslovakia's position as an industrial powerhouse producing materiel for the Nazi war effort. Only when the Third Reich tottered towards collapse, and American and Soviet boots advanced onto Czech soil in 1945, did the Czechs of Prague dare to defy their Nazi conquerors again.

Though it is doubtful Czechoslovakia could have mustered the strength to throw off the grip of Hitler's colossal war machine earlier than mid-1945, it is equally clear that the assassination failed to inspire significant resistance and resulted in its temporary suppression.

Having failed to alter the course of the war itself, the Final Solution (other than perhaps to hasten it), or the Czech resistance (save to weaken it through liquidation and terror), it is still fair to ask what the assassination of Reinhard Heydrich achieved. Since the Allies would certainly have hanged the Gestapo general at Nuremberg following the war if he survived that long, the bold, daring, and courageously executed plan resulted in one deeply tragic consequence: pointlessly trading the lives of some 5,000 Czechs and perhaps thousands of Jews for a single German life doomed sooner or later regardless of the plot's outcome.

On top of all that, Czech territory was also used during the Holocaust. A prison on the outskirts of Prague, at Terezín, was built as a concentration camp for Czechoslovak Jews and predominantly employed as a transit point on the way to the gas chambers of Auschwitz.[64]

Tito's Yugoslavia

"Comrade Khrushchev often repeats that Socialism cannot be built with American wheat. I think it can be done by anyone who knows how to do it, while a person who doesn't know how to

---

[64] Ed Vulliamy, "Terezín: 'The music connected us to the lives we had lost'", *The Guardian*, 5 April 2013, https://www.theguardian.com/music/2013/apr/05/terezin-nazi-camp-music-eva-clarke, [accessed 10 April 2019]

do it cannot build Socialism even with his own wheat. Khrushchev says we live on charity received from the imperialist countries … What moral right have those who attack us to rebuke us about American aid or credits when Khruschev himself has just tried to conclude an economic agreement with America?" - Tito

Following the end of World War II, the Yugoslav Army (formerly the Partisans) executed tens of thousands of their adversaries, including former Chetniks, Ustashe, and others. Mihailovic himself fell into Yugoslavian hands, and the Yugoslavs executed him in 1946. This, of course, also had the fringe benefit of eliminating many people who might have objected strenuously to the establishment of a communist state.

Tito, riding a wave of triumph and military glory, brazenly engineered the takeover of the nation by his party, the People's Front, in late 1945. Though Yugoslavia held elections on November 27th, 1945, Tito loaded the ballot-boxes in his favor by declaring that large lists of people could not vote due to supposed collaboration with the Germans. In fact, the list consisted mostly of people believed to be anti-communist, with no reference in most cases to any real connection with the Germans.

Since he had effectively declared that only Partisans and their known supporters could vote, Tito engineered a 90% victory for the People's Front. With his party now immovably in power, Tito abolished the monarchy just two days after the general election, and King Petar II Karadjordjevic fled to the United States, where he died in 1970.

King Petar II

Initially, Yugoslavia showed itself to be a ferociously Marxist state, with a secret police, purges of dissenters, numerous arrests, and suppression of religion in the name of communist atheism. Catholic Archbishop Alois Stepinac received a prison sentence of 16 years for alleged

Ustashe activity, though the communists steadily reduced his sentence later. The Archbishop's imprisonment caused the Pope to excommunicate Tito.

Tito's communist party also took over most of the major industries immediately. Tito launched a Five-Year Plan for rapid economic expansion. The CPY expropriated huge amounts of private property. Any factory that worked even a single day during the war years received the label of a "collaborating" business and fell to automatic expropriation by the state. Next, Tito's government seized all property and factories belonging to foreigners, including Yugoslav allies such as the British and Soviets.

The First Five-Year Plan rolled an incredible 27% of Yugoslavia's gross national product back into economic development, 92% of it industrial. This outdid the scope of even the Soviet Union's Five-Year Plans, and caused considerable hardship to large sectors of the populace as production of food and consumer goods dropped to build up a stock of capital goods (manufacturing machinery).

Initially, Tito's slightly unique take on Marxism won praise from the Soviets, as a 1947 article indicated: "The concrete embodiment of the ideas of Marxism regarding the unity of the working class with the majority of working people [...] has been most consistently developed in Yugoslavia where the People's Front unites almost seven million people [...] The People's Front [...] is a social-political organisation of the people in which the working class, headed by the Communist Party, plays a leading role." (Swain, 2011, 90).

However, Yugoslavia soon split with Stalin and the USSR due to Tito's maverick leadership. Tito, in a bid to assist a communist revolution in Greece, effectively invaded Albanian territory to protect Greek communist bases there, without first consulting or even informing either Stalin or Albania's leader Enver Hoxha. Though the Soviets eventually outwardly accepted this action, they began pressuring Tito to add Yugoslavia to a planned Balkan Federation. The Federation, under Soviet control, would effectively reduce all of the member countries, Yugoslavia included, to the helpless provinces of what might be called a "greater Soviet empire." An exchange of letters followed, in which Stalin claimed that the Yugoslavian success in World War II stemmed entirely from the Red Army. In fact, this represented a complete falsehood; the Yugoslavian Partisans largely won the war in their own country independently, while most of what aid they did receive came from the British, not the Soviets, whose support always appeared lukewarm.

The communist Cominform convened in Bucharest on June 28th, 1948 and expelled Yugoslavia from its fold. Though it issued an invitation to Tito and his top lieutenants to attend, Tito refused to travel there, noting "if we have to be killed, we'll be killed on our own soil." (Swain, 2011, 96). That was a clear insight, given Stalin's long history of summoning people to areas he controlled in order to have them killed.

Thus, for several months, Yugoslavia existed in a sort of vacuum, with the Soviet Union looming over it in wrath. Tito already looked towards the Americans, perplexed by the entire affair, to save him from the USSR, declaring, "The Americans are not fools. They won't let the Russians reach the Adriatic." (Banac, 1988, 137). This essentially encapsulated Tito's foreign and domestic policy for the rest of his reign as Yugoslavia's dictatorial president – maintaining a species of communist state while relying on tacit Western support to keep the Soviet juggernaut at bay. Edvard Kardelj, Yugoslavia's Foreign Minister, provided a succinct summary of how his nation could maintain itself as an unaligned state between the two vast power blocs of the 20th century, the free world to the west and the communist world to the east, by leveraging the "tendency among the imperialists to exploit the contradictions between the socialist states, very much in the same way as we wish to exploit the internal contradictions of the imperialist system." (Banac, 1988, 138),

Kardelj

The U.S. and England cautiously adopted a "wedge strategy" towards Yugoslavia, supporting it in order to keep it out of the Soviet sphere of influence and put up a roadblock in the way of Stalin's European ambitions. Tito accordingly ceased giving aid to the Greek communist organizations, paid back U.S. Lend-Lease aid, and remunerated English and American people whose property in Yugoslavia had suffered expropriation. Still, the Americans naturally remained cautious of Tito's and Yugoslavia's intentions. They also could not quite decide how to deal with a country that housed a repressive, dictatorial Marxist regime, yet showed strong signs of nationalism and showed itself willing to defy the still-ascendant power of Moscow. As George Frost Kennan, an influential Cold War political strategist, said of Yugoslavia, a "new factor of fundamental and profound significance has been introduced into the world communist movement by the demonstration that the Kremlin can be successfully defied by one of its own minions (Lees, 1997, 54). By 1955, the US government had given Tito more than $1.2 billion in combined economic and military aid. The English also provided assistance, though on a lesser scale due to their waning power.

Tito's regime gradually moved away from a purely communist approach as the pragmatic demands of survival placed effectiveness ahead of ideology. The Yugoslavians tried a three-year trial period of collective farms, or SRZs, after which they asked the peasants if they wished to stay or leave. Flooded with gigantic numbers of requests to leave, Tito and his cabinet decided to return 1.5 million acres of agricultural land to individual peasant family ownership in 1952. Collective farming vanished in most areas by 1953, with a few notable exceptions.

At around the same time, the Yugoslavian state developed one of its other unique characteristics, the principle of self-management. Under this scheme, many factories worked not at the direction of a cumbersome and dangerous central bureaucracy as in the case of the Soviet Union, but by "workers' councils" elected and staffed by the laborers at the factory themselves.

Showing considerable acuity, Tito declared in 1950 that the USSR actually represented a counterrevolutionary state. Stalin, he said, operated the entire Soviet Union as a gigantic capitalist monopoly. His method, he claimed, placed the means of production into the hands of those Marx intended: the workers themselves. When the West invented the term "Titoism" to describe Tito's rule in Yugoslavia, by contrast, Tito claimed that he represented the true Marxist and that Stalin was the "heretic:" "It is simply that we have added nothing to Marxist-Leninist doctrine. [...] Should 'Titoism' become an ideological line, we would become revisionist; we would have renounced Marxism. We are Marxists, I am a Marxist and therefore I cannot be a 'Titoist.' Stalin is the revisionist: it is he who has wandered from the Marxist road. 'Titoism' as a doctrine does not exist." (Dedijer, 1953, 432).

This, of course, represented something of a semantic dodge, unlike Tito's insightful remark that Soviet communism resembled a gigantic monopolistic corporation. Yugoslavia under Tito matched no other state on the planet. Soon, the workers' councils at the factories received permission to make investments and other business decisions, using the funds their efforts earned, independent of state interference, provided that "ownership" remained divided equally between everyone who worked at the factory and decisions occurred by vote rather than "board of directors" fiat.

On the personal scale, Tito's success with women continued. The Yugoslavian leader met a nurse, Jovanka Budisavljevic, after a gall bladder operation and married her in 1951. Jovanka remained married to Tito for the next 29 years until he died, though their relationship broke down to some degree several years before his death. Jovanka lived until 2013, witnessing both the entirety of Tito's reign and the significant events of the post-Tito era.

Dragan Zebeljan's picture of Jovanka

Stalin's death in 1953 while Tito was visiting Britain represented a major change in Soviet leadership. Tito attempted rapprochement with the Soviet Union, only to be largely rebuffed by new Soviet leader Nikita Khrushchev. However, in 1955, Khrushchev visited Belgrade, and, after reaching something of an understanding with Tito, both men signed the Belgrade Declaration. This promulgated an agreement of mutual non-interference, and Khrushchev canceled all of Yugoslavia's debts upon his return to the Soviet Union.

Khrushchev

Tito felt safe enough to visit Moscow in 1956, and Khrushchev and Tito continued their diplomatic dance for the rest of the decade, but Yugoslavia – in the person of its leader – steadfastly refused any agreement that would reduce the country's independence. Tito continued playing the East and West off against each other in order to keep his own country essentially safe from major external interference throughout the 1950s.

Tito continued to enjoy the high life as he aged, living in superbly furnished castles, supplying himself with every luxury, and continuing to pursue women besides his wife Jovanka. However, he also continued to pay attention to running his unusual state and addressing problems as they arose. In the early 1960s, the self-management program ran into problems due to the difficulties of allotting investment funds. Officials managed to take over the distribution of these funds, compromising the independence of many self-managed factories. This led to the production of unnecessary or substandard goods as the officials pursued their own agendas without reference to market demand.

Tito in 1961

At the same time, consumer demand burgeoned as the economy recovered and the self-management program produced genuinely effective economic activity. Tito waffled for some time, apparently trying to coordinate his efforts with Khrushchev, but the latter's fall removed the likelihood of any cooperation between the Yugoslavian and Soviet economies that would not leave Moscow with the whip hand and strip Tito of his independence.

At the Eighth Party Congress in 1965, Tito increased the amount of money that self-managed factories could retain for investment to 70%, up from the current 30%, thus improving the economic position of the workers and attempting to reduce the power of the officials to interfere in the economy's functioning. The bureaucracy naturally resisted this, wishing to retain its control over investment and thus economic planning and activity.

Tito returned to a measure of centralization in the final decade of his life. Though self-management remained a key portion of the Yugoslavian economy, the 1974 Constitution made the state's structure much more hierarchal, giving Tito the power to resist change and try to keep his creation as an unchanging structure for the rest of his life. The Constitution also named Tito president for life in its first article.

Tito continued to enjoy his extravagant lifestyle during the final decade of his life. However, he no longer had the energy of youth and his infinitely complex system began to ossify without his constant tinkering and guidance. The dissident Milovan Djilas noted, "In the late 1960s, Yugoslavia had another chance, the most promising if also the most uncertain, at democratisation … [but by] the early 1970s Tito more firmly than ever held back the movement for change; he forced creative social, national and individual potentialities to revert to the withered ideals of his youth." (Swain, 2011, 189). Nevertheless, Yugoslavia enjoyed nearly first-world standards of living and a unique system of "self-management" that did not match either communist or capitalist designs. Regardless of its flaws and Tito's human failings, Josip Broz had created a relatively prosperous state that remained separate from the problems of other Cold War countries east or west.

Tito died in early 1980 at 88 years of age, killed by gangrene caused by a leg amputation following arterial blockage. An enormous number of heads of state, including 31 presidents and four kings, attended the funeral of the Croatian machinist who had witnessed and participated in the most tumultuous events of the 20th century.

The 1980s

Tito's death was certain to create a power vacuum in Yugoslavia. He had attempted to stabilize the country's politics with a new constitution in 1974 that set out a collective, rotating leadership, but he also failed to appoint a political successor. The settlement worked for a few years, but several shocks, political and economic, caused fault lines to appear, and these issues worsened as politicians started to agitate nationalist bases in the 1980s. The end of the Cold War further weakened Yugoslavia, leading the country to the brink of disaster.

In fact, as soon as Tito died in 1980, nationalist émigré groups were hailing, predicting or calling for the demise of Yugoslavia.[65] Several countries were home to significant expatriate groups, particularly the Croat organizations. The first actual post-Tito unrest, however, took

---

[65] John R. Lampe, *Yugoslavia as History: Twice there was a country* (Cambridge: Cambridge University Press, 2000), p. 299.

place in Kosovo in 1981. Ethnic Albanian groups, particularly students, protested against a range of issues, including history teaching and using the Albanian language. The subsequent riots disturbed the elites in Belgrade, as well as the minority Serbs in Kosovo.[66] The province's place in Serb history gave it particular significance as the birthplace of a conscious Serb nation, following their battle with the invading Ottomans in 1389. That Serbs may be losing their privileged position in the province, or even being threatened or persecuted by ethnic Albanians, led to acute sensitivity. A trend missing during the years of the socialist Federation was Serb nationalism. When it returned, the edifices holding Yugoslavia together began to crumble.

It was something altogether less emotive that first debilitated Yugoslavia in the post-Tito years: the economy. It may appear as if the state only faltered after Tito's death, but the 1980s were in fact the fruition of many of the dictator's policies. Tito had allowed Yugoslavia to live beyond its means for years and acquired a liking for foreign debt. He was somewhat different from his peers because he effectively shared income with his people. However, when Western banks had to contend with high interest rates in the late 1970s and early 1980s, pressure was inevitably passed on to debtors, including Yugoslavia. By 1983, the country was in serious economic trouble.

The impact of Yugoslavia's economic frailty was not immediately obvious. The country successfully hosted the 1984 Winter Olympic Games in Sarajevo, glorifying in its mantra of brotherhood and multinational and multi-religious harmony.[67] By this time, however, the Federation lacked any substantial figures. In many ways, in the mid-1980s, it resembled other Central European and Eastern European countries, as party functionaries in bland suits talked about unlikely production targets and factory output. This political impotence and latent economic problems – high inflation, low productivity, high debt and need for hard currency – would culminate in the horrors of the 1990s' conflicts when exploited by nationalists. Initially, however, the nationalist impulse was one of self-preservation by weak communist politicians. The most notable – or infamous - example of a career communist who turned to nationalism during the decade was Slobodan Milošević.

---

[66] Carole Rogel, *The Breakup of Yugoslavia and its Aftermath* (London: Greenwood Press, 2004), p. 17.

[67] Zlatko Jovanovic, 'The 1984 Sarajevo Winter Olympics and Identity-Formation in Late Socialist Sarajevo', *The International Journal of the History of Sport* (34:9, 2017, pp. 767-782).

Milošević

Slobodan Milošević was born in 1941 in Serbia, then occupied by the Nazis during the Second World War. He became active in the Yugoslav Communist Party youth section during the 1960s while he was at university in Belgrade. At this time, he became acquainted with Ivan Stambolić, whose uncle Petar Stambolić was a key member of the Serbian communist executive.

Starting in local politics, Milošević worked his way up to prominence in Serbian politics by the 1980s. Yugoslavia may have been nominally an egalitarian socialist state, but connections were often important in career progression. Milošević had essentially been mentored by Ivan Stambolić and, using his uncle, began to scale the ladder of Yugoslav communism. Interestingly, in light of later events, Stambolić was considered a "liberal" within the spectrum of Yugoslav politics. By the time of his death in 2006, Milošević had made a reputation with his own particularly virulent form of nationalism, far from the communism of fraternity and brotherhood he embraced in his youth.

By 1984, he had been elevated to a leadership position in Belgrade, and in 1986 Milošević was voted President of the Serbian League of Communists. The structures of Yugoslav politics were complex and multi-layered, but essentially each republic had its own parliament and leadership which then appointed a delegate to the rotating central committee. Thus, by 1986, Milošević was in a position of some influence in Serb politics, the biggest of the Yugoslav republics, but as he moved into power, the direction of Serb society was taking a radical shift. Since the 1930s, it had been accepted that Serb nationalism would be lethal to the Yugoslav project, so for 50 years Tito and his successors had worked to satisfy the various republics and nationalities without allowing Serbs to dominate the Federation. This was, of course, difficult since Serbia was the most populous component part of Yugoslavia. This fragile, but successful, bargain lasted until the mid-1980s, when a number of Serb academics attempted to revise, or revisit, the country's history.

In 1986, the notorious SANU (translated as the Serbian Academy of Sciences) memorandum was published. The document, written by a number of academics and thinkers, aired several long-standing, suppressed Serb grievances.[68] It claimed that Edvard Kardelj (identified as a "Slovene") and Tito (a "Slovene" and a "Croat") had colluded in an attempt to keep the Serbs in a position of relative weakness in Yugoslavia. The document cited the position of Kosovo and its decoupling from Serbia in the 1974 constitution, a situation that enraged Serb national sentiment.[69] SANU berated the role of "fascist" Croats, both during the Second World War and afterwards. It revisited the old theme of centralization of power (favored by Serbs) and devolution (preferred by most of the republics). The SANU memorandum included contributions from 1960s-era Praxis intellectuals. Back in the turmoil of the 1960s, writers such as Mihailo Marković were considered reformers, but by the mid-1980s they had morphed into purveyors of virulent Serb nationalism, while Yugoslav communists, including Serbs like Ivan Stambolić, condemned the document.

It was into this background that Milošević stepped. As Serbian Communist Party chief from 1986, he certainly would have felt pressure at home to take a more assertive approach in his dealings with the other republics. He also may have seen the opportunity to garner and solidify support within Serbia by asserting nationalist claims. It was exactly this dynamic that other Yugoslav leaders had attempted to curtail as far back as the 1930s. Slobodan Milošević would eventually go down the path towards national chauvinism. The first real opportunity he had to state his nationalist credentials was over Kosovo. The Serb nation had eulogized the role the "Field of Blackbirds" had played in defining who the Serbs were, and this battlefield, in Kosovo, had been the place where Serbs had resisted Ottoman marauders all the way back in 1389. Therefore, Serb nationalists were unhappy when Tito separated Kosovo from the Serbian Yugoslav republic in his 1974 constitution.

Ironically, the document was an attempt to decentralise power in Yugoslavia and dilute the kind of nationalist agitation seen during the Croatian Spring, which lasted from 1968-1971. By the 1980s, Kosovo was inhabited by a majority (90%) of ethnic Albanians and a minority (approximately 10%) of Serbs. The former had demonstrated in 1981, demanding greater recognition of the Albanian language and historical tradition in education. The authorities had

[68] Laura Silber and Allan Little, *The Death of Yugoslavia* (London: Penguin, 1995), p. 31; 'SANU Memorandum', http://central.gutenberg.org/articles/SANU_Memorandum, (accessed 7 January 2016)

[69] Carole Rogel, *The Breakup of Yugoslavia and its Aftermath* (London: Greenwood Press, 2004), pp. 16-17.

cracked down severely on these demonstrations, but the episode made clear that the Kosovo issues were likely to come up again at a later date.

In 1987, it was the turn of the Serbs in Kosovo to protest. Demonstrating against alleged persecution by ethnic-Albanians, the Serbs demanded action and protection from the (predominantly ethnic Albanian) police force.[70] Their calls were answered by an unlikely source: Milošević himself. The Serb President, Ivan Stambolić, decided to start a dialogue with the protestors and despatched his trusted lieutenant Milošević to Kosovo. Milošević gave an apparently impassioned plea against nationalism in Kosovo, although he initially appeared unwilling to meet with the local Serb protestors.[71] Nevertheless, after complaints from some Serbs, he agreed to meet the nationalists against the orders of Stambolić. Milošević's stance clearly changed as he decided to explicitly back the Serb nationalists, enraging Yugoslav communists across the Federation. Still in Kosovo, at a meeting with the Serbs expressing their grievances, Milošević was informed that police were beating demonstrators on the streets. Going to the scene of the alleged violence, Milošević asserted, "No one shall dare beat you again!" Broadcast across state television that evening, Milošević became, almost by accident, the defender of the Serbs. He would cultivate this image remorselessly over the next 15 years.

---

[70] *The Sydney Morning Herald*, 'The rise and fall of Milošević', 12 March 2006, https://www.smh.com.au/world/the-rise-and-fall-of-Milošević-20060312-gdn4y1.html [accessed 30 October 2018]
[71] Laura Silber and Allan Little, *The Death of Yugoslavia* (London: Penguin, 1996)

Stambolić

As Milošević sought to increase his personal power in Belgrade, Stambolić attempted to discipline Milošević, grievously concerned over Yugoslavia's fate if his deputy continued along a nationalist path. A public criticism was delivered to Milošević on state news, but this elicited a fiery response. Milošević accumulated support for his nationalist approach towards Kosovo and began to undermine Stambolić. Dragiša Pavlović, a Stambolić ally, was expelled from the Communist Party over his attitude towards Kosovo. Milošević claimed that Pavlović was soft on Albanian radicals, and Milošević also began to install loyalists into bureaucratic and advisory positions. Stambolić himself was then sacked, nominally because of a letter he had written in support of Pavlović, but in reality as a political power grab by Milošević, who succeeded him as

President of Serbia within the Yugoslav Federation. In 1988-1989, Milošević launched his so-called "anti-bureaucratic revolution" which mostly entailed removing the old guard and putting his allies into power in Vojvodina, Kosovo and Montenegro.[72] In a remarkably short space of time, Milošević had transformed himself from a dull party functionary into a Serb nationalist capable of overturning the ruling elites in the surrounding republics and accruing ever more personal power and influence.

Many books about the fall of Yugoslavia emphasize the role played by the end of the Cold War from 1989-1991, but it is important to recognise that nationalist agitation had already started to surge in Yugoslavia while the status quo in Central Europe and Eastern Europe still existed. The winds of Gorbachev's *Glasnost* – or openness – reforms blew across the communist world during this time, and a desire for greater freedom in many countries led to the overthrow of the authorities in favor of democracy and market capitalism. In Yugoslavia, the desire for greater personal autonomy seamlessly transformed into group demands, essentially national self-determination. This proved intractable since the different peoples of Yugoslavia did not live in discrete territories, and also because several of these prerogatives lent on a maximalist claim of a "Greater Croatia," a "Greater Serbia," and so on. The umbrella of socialism suppressed, for the most part, national competition in the Yugoslav Federation, which had always existed but had simply been dormant.

The growing sense of Serb domination in Yugoslavia, particularly under the aegis of Milošević, concerned the other republics. In February 1989, Slovenian leader Milan Kučan stormed out of a central committee meeting in protest. Kučan's subsequent speech defended the rights of ethnic Albanians in Kosovo, as well as his own people's autonomy, the Slovenes. Deemed inflammatory, this brought Serb protestors out onto the streets of Belgrade. Shortly afterwards, the Kosovo and Vojvodina assemblies were forced to accept constitutional changes that increased Belgrade's influence over their affairs. The short-lived period, after 1974, of greater autonomy for these two republics was over.

---

[72] John B. Allcock, *Explaining Yugoslavia* (London: Hurst & Company, 2000), p. 427.

Kučan

Milošević continued to set about consolidating his own prestige amongst the Serbs. On June 28, 1989, marking the 600th anniversary of the Battle of Kosovo, Milošević spoke to a million Serbs at a rally on the Polje battlefield itself.

Serbia was not the only Yugoslav republic to see a rise in nationalism in the 1980s. Almost across the board, nationalist sentiment grew in Yugoslavia in the decade after Tito died. The geopolitical importance of Yugoslavia declined as the West and the Soviets under Gorbachev moved towards a new détente after 1985, and there were the economic factors that eroded Yugoslav's living standards and led to a loss of faith in the federal system. One could point to structural flaws in the whole Yugoslav project, and that the country's history after 1918 had been a series of short term measures to prevent an inevitable dissolution. Nevertheless, putting all these structural factors to one side, individuals, personalities, and human agency were clearly crucial in undermining the legitimacy of socialist Yugoslavia.

First and foremost was the role played by Milošević, but other republics also played their part. In Croatia, the independently-minded group of intellectuals and agitators who rose to prominence in the Croatian Spring had been imprisoned, expelled from influential positions, or sidelined after 1971. This most likely hardened the positions of many Croat nationalists in favor of total separation from Yugoslavia. Backed by a large diaspora, particularly in the Federal

Republic of Germany, émigré groups and a considerable funding apparatus, the support network was already in place for any move towards greater autonomy for Croatia.

This was embodied in the late 1980s by Franjo Tudjman.[73] An academic and Croat cultural nationalist, Tudjman had played a key role in the 1960s' disturbances, only to have been stripped of his military rank and imprisoned on more than one occasion after the Croatian Spring. Tudjman, however, was a hugely controversial figure.[74] In the 1980s, he started to articulate the fixtures and fittings of a Croatian state. These included the flag from the Ustaše era. Having brutally committed ethnic cleansing against the Serbs during its time in power between 1941-1945, invoking the Ustaše was an inflammatory, ill-judged move. Around 12% of Croatia's population, almost 600,000 people, were ethnic Serbs, and it is not difficult to imagine how any invocation of Ustaše or the NDH (referring to the wartime, proto-fascist Independent State of Croatia) regime invoked terror and horrific memories within those communities. In response, Serb nationalist intellectuals branded Croats part of a "genocidal nation."[75]

Franjo Tudjman

Slovenia, under Milan Kučan, also moved towards autonomy in the 1980s. Feeding on sentiment across the communist world, Slovenian media called for greater democratization and respect for human rights after 1987.[76] Kučan also took his controversial stance towards Kosovo,

[73] Carole Rogel, *The Breakup of Yugoslavia and its Aftermath* (London: Greenwood Press, 2004), pp. 141-142.
[74] Carole Rogel, *The Breakup of Yugoslavia and its Aftermath* (London: Greenwood Press, 2004), p. 142.
[75] Vesna Drapac, *Constructing Yugoslavia: A Transnational History*, (Basingstoke: Palgrave Macmillan, 2010), p. 250.
[76] Viktor Meier, *Yugoslavia. A History of its Demise*, translated by Sabrina Ramet, (London: Routledge, 1995), p. 59.

which set Slovenia against the Serbs and Milošević. Slovenia was the most economically developed part of Yugoslavia and was confident it could prosper alone. It also did not share a border with Serbia, and it was relatively homogeneous ethnically (meaning it did not contain a big contingent of any other Yugoslav national minority), potentially shielding it from aggression. Once Yugoslavia began to destabilize after 1987, Slovenia saw its opportunity to break away. Kučan presented himself as a civilized democrat and the voice of reason, and clearly Slovenia's path to independence was markedly different than other republics. Thus, in his own way, Kučan played a key part in the breakup of Yugoslavia.[77]

Meanwhile, nationalist leaders had moved towards positions of influence in other parts of the Federation, such as Bosnian Serb leader Radovan Karadžić, who formed the Serb Democratic Party (SDS) in 1989.

Despite the issues, at the end of the 1980s, the fragile peace in Yugoslavia still held. It was in the economic sphere that the country appeared to be fraying.

Communist Rule in Czechoslovakia

In the wake of World War II, Czechoslovakia was essentially returned to its constitutional status quo, albeit without its ethnic Germans. Beneš was President once more and Tomáš Masaryk's son Jan became Foreign Minister.

Beneš' hope was that his country would act as a bridge between east and west, in keeping with Czechoslovakia's position in the heart of Europe. It is perhaps unsurprising that Beneš wanted to adopt a hedged position after he had been sold out by his Western backers in 1938. At this stage, however, as the Cold War took shape in the late 1940s, neutrality was not an option. It may have been the kind of position that Tito's Yugoslavia would excel at as leader of the Non-Aligned Movement, but for Czechoslovakia, at this point, it was untenable. As a result, Prague swiftly fell under the orbit of their "liberators," the Soviet Union.

Some Czechoslovaks were only too happy to participate in this shift. In elections held in 1946, socialists and communists did particularly well and took up positions in the cabinet. A communist, Klement Gottwald, was named Prime Minister in July 1946.

Tensions between the United States and the Soviet Union, and their respective allies, worsened in 1946 and 1947. The Truman administration offered European countries "Marshall Aid" as a means of rebuilding their shattered economies in return for closer relations with Washington. Beneš was keen on the idea, but Moscow adamantly opposed and intervened in 1947. The writing was again on the wall for Beneš - having watched as his country was overrun by fascists in the 1930s, he was now about to watch history repeat itself, this time by communists, in the

---

[77] John R. Lampe, *Yugoslavia as History. Twice there was a country.* (Cambridge: Cambridge University Press, 2000), pp. 332.

1940s.

Gottwald's popularity, as well as his Communist Party, had declined during his time in office, and it was expected that he would suffer at the next election, but that election would never take place. Gottwald, in league with the Soviets, essentially conducted a coup d'état, a communist takeover, in 1948. Jan Masaryk, not a communist, died mysteriously in February 1948, found dead afte having apparently jumped from a window at the Foreign Ministry. Next, Beneš stepped down, allowing Gottwald to ascend to the presidency.[78] Beneš died in September 1948, traumatized by the vandalism of the opponents to his multinational, liberal vision of Czechoslovakia.

With Gottwald in power, the country soon came in line behind Moscow, joining the Comecon - the USSR's communist collective - in 1949, and then the Warsaw Pact, a collective security instrument, in 1955. The Iron Curtain that divided Europe during the Cold War had come down with Czechoslovakia on the front line, but just inside the communist bloc. It would take 50 years before the barriers came down.[79]

With communism as the official ideology in Czechoslovakia, Czech and Slovak nationalism were severely repressed, though the two constituent parts were permitted separate communist parties. In fact, during the 1950s, the country grew impressively despite its conversion to the orthodox communism that prevailed in the region. Demonstrations broke out in Plzeň in 1953 as part of the protests across the communist world (ostensibly against agricultural reforms), but these were violently suppressed. Anti-government sentiment was subdued for a decade until a series of economic and political reforms in the 1960s which would inculcate the eventual forces that would force Czechoslovakia apart.

Antonín Josef Novotný replaced Gottwald in 1953 as General Secretary of Czechoslovakia's Communist Party, making him leader of the country. Following the pattern seen in many of the communist dictatorships in Central Europe and Eastern Europe, Czechoslovakia experienced periods of some economic growth then stagnation. The 1950s were relatively successful for the country, but this fell back in the 1960s. Soviet leader Nikita Khrushchev oversaw a thaw in the economic and political straightjacket imposed by most communist states from the mid-1950s, and although the USSR reverted to a more closed model after Khrushchev was pushed aside in 1964, other members of the communist bloc experimented with reforms during this period.

In Czechoslovakia, this took the form of the "New Economic Model" in 1965, which made some attempt at broad-based reform, as well as some economic liberalisation. What started as modest reforms—essentially an attempt to increase economic activity—opened a Pandora's Box

---

[78] BBC, "Soviet power in Eastern Europe", https://www.bbc.com/bitesize/guides/z9wxj6f/revision/2, [accessed 10 April 2019]

[79] Godfrey Hodgson, *People's Century: From the dawn of the century to the eve of the millennium* (Godalming: BBC Books, 1998)

of pent-up frustration. The results would have a long-lasting impact on the integrity of the Czechoslovak dual-national project.

In 1968 Novotný stood down and was replaced by the head of the Slovak Communist Party, Alexander Dubček. It was an appointment that was to have far-reaching effects for Czechoslovakia, the Cold War and even the stability of the communist bloc. Dubček quickly set about building upon the faint shards of light promised by the 1965 economic reforms. In what was called the "Prague Spring," Dubček famously said that he was overseeing "socialism with a human face."

Dubček and his allies were essentially trying to reform the communist system through increased democracy within a one-party state, reducing censorship in the press, radio, and television by encouraging dialogue. Cultural exploits such as music, art and poetry blossomed, and Czechs and Slovaks, previously buttoned-up, suddenly felt emboldened to air their grievances. Of course, the grievances were widespread, especially in 1968, a year of revolution across much of the world. Students organised across the country in a similar fashion as others across Europe, and this liberalization grievously worried the Soviet leadership and other communist dictatorships.[80]

In retrospect, it was only a matter of time before Moscow intervened. The USSR and the Warsaw Pact viewed the Prague Spring as an existential threat to its influence in the region, and in late August 1968, the Soviets sent troops into Czechoslovakia to reassert control over the country. The Warsaw Pact forces were met with bitterness by the Czechoslovaks, who resisted the invasion without resorting to violence. Dubček was summoned to Moscow, where he was forced to explain himself in a humiliating meeting. He was detained in Moscow before being sent back to his occupied country and stripped of his authority.

The harsh response to the Prague Spring was met with both support and criticism from other communist countries. Nicolae Ceaușescu, for instance, then a reformer in Romania but later a megalomaniac tyrant, made a speech in Bucharest's Palace Square denouncing the invasion as a "grave danger to peace in Europe, to the fate of socialism in the world."[81] Ceaușescu repeatedly expressed his support for the Czechoslovak communists that very nearly put him on his own collision course with Moscow. The Romanian leader was cunning enough to use the crisis to his advantage by rousing nationalist sentiment for an unwieldy outside power. This would be a core driving force in the eventual decline of communism, as reform often became intertwined with nationalism.

Yugoslavia's autocrat, Josif Broz Tito, would be another who tentatively came out in favor of Dubček, likely because he was under pressure from his own domestic protests. Yugoslavia was

---

[80] Jussi M. Hanhimaki, *The Rise and Fall of Détente. American Foreign Policy and the Transformation of the Cold War* (Washington DC: Potomac Books)

[81] Misha Glenny, *The Balkans 1804-2012: Nationalism, War and the Great Powers* (London: Granta, 2012), p. 594.

in some ways comparable with Czechoslovakia, as both were formed at the end of the First World War and represented multiethnic confederations. Both had been invaded by the Nazis during the 1930s and 1940s, both initially were sponsored by Britain and France, and both were abandoned in the face of fascism. The governments in Prague and Belgrade were therefore highly sensitive to questions about their own security, and although both states were now under the umbrella of Moscow and the communist bloc, the passions of their people were quickly aroused when it became obvious that their autonomy was only superficial. Ultimately, however, both Czechoslovakia (explicitly) and Yugoslavia (implicitly) were forced to kowtow to the Soviets in 1968 and in the aftermath. This was to cause deep resentment, particularly for the Czechoslovaks, and the anger would fester for another 20 years before the Soviet Union finally collapsed. For Czechoslovakia, the nationalism that was stirred by these events would lead to a peaceful separation in 1993, but for Yugoslavia, it would result in the bloodiest conflict in Europe since the Second World War.

1968 had another impact on Czechoslovakia, and that was the constant issue of its alliances, the matter that had so animated the state's founders. Reluctant participants in the Warsaw Pact that had now attacked them, the Czechoslovaks desperately called for assistance from other communist countries, and even to the West. The major democratic powers all considered coming to Prague's aid, but all had their own imbroglios. France was in the midst of its own insurrection, and the French elite were terrified they were about to see a revolution. Also riven by strife, the Johnson administration in the United States was mired in the Vietnam War and desperate to come to some kind of arrangement with the major communist powers to extricate itself from the war. The last thing it wanted was to be drawn into yet another communist dispute. Britain was more self-conscious of its failings a generation earlier, so it offered little other than voicing support.

During 1968, Czechoslovak communists had shown themselves to be open to political reform. Alexander Dubček's reforms led to an unprecedented degree of openness and dialogue, as well as greater political discourse and freedom of expression. His removal from office in April 1969 was a hammer blow to liberals across Central Europe and Eastern Europe, particularly as the occupation elicited no response from the West or NATO.

By this point, however, Yugoslavia, which was also experiencing demonstrations, became concerned it could be invaded by the Soviets. Moscow wanted to avoid another of its clients taking an independent path, as Yugoslavia had done in 1948 when Tito left Comecon and pursued an autonomous path beyond the clutches of Stalin, so subsequent bouts of unrest and demands for reform in East Berlin in 1953 and Hungary in 1956 had been met with Soviet military force and occupation.[82] The Soviets, now led by Leonid Brezhnev, resorted to similar tactics in 1968.

---

[82] Mary Fulbrook, *History of Germany, 1918-2000: the divided nation* (Oxford: Blackwell, 2002)

Czechoslovakia had challenged Soviet hegemony within the country and the region, and the Soviets would not accept another Yugoslavia, but those heady days of the Prague Spring would long be remembered in Czechoslovakia. As was proven in the 1980s, reform of the command and control system of communist, one-party rule was almost impossible. In fact, Mikhail Gorbachev claimed to be an unreconstructed communist up to the end of the USSR despite having initiated political liberalization, and the Czechoslovaks would find out shortly after the final act for the communist bloc that a country without a common enemy, and with true accountability to its people, would prove a very tricky proposition. Keeping together a multinational state without a shared history would be beyond the leaders of the 1990s, many of whom cut their political teeth in the protests and struggles of the 1970s and 1980s after the Prague Spring. Furthermore, whereas many political systems posit liberalism and nationalism at either ends of their spectrum, for reformers in Central Europe and Eastern Europe, the two forces would merge. This was very much in keeping with 19th century liberals involved in national independent movements, such as in Italy and Germany, and the manner in which they did so would be crucial to the eventual split in Czechoslovakia.

The major figure to emerge in the 1970s was Václav Havel, a liberal who urged the continuing union of Czechs and Slovaks. Ultimately, he would be outflanked by more nationally inclined liberals, but not before he had helped overthrow the communist regime. Havel was born in 1936 in Prague to a well-off family, but by the time Havel became interested in the 1950s, his family background was frowned upon, deemed too bourgeois and liberal. The Sudeten Germans had by then been expelled from the state, and Havel later enraged Czech nationalists with his conciliatory approach to the ethnic Germans.

The young man also harbored a creativity that had difficulty expressing itself in the closed environment of communist Czechoslovakia. As a result, Havel started to work in the theater and soon began writing his own plays. His first full-length play, *The Garden Party*, was shown in 1963, and he received acclaim during the decade, with his work even being performed in the United States. The Prague Spring was an ideal background for someone like Havel when artistic work suddenly became *de rigueur*, but this came to a crashing halt when the Soviets invaded in August 1968.

Havel was active in peacefully protesting the occupation, appearing on Radio Free Czechoslovakia to oppose the invasion, and this marked him out as a dissident. Thus, when the dust had settled, Havel was blacklisted and his plays were banned. This meant he found work difficult to come by, but, as was often the case, suppressing his voice only made it more determined. During the 1970s, Havel was forced underground, but he coalesced around other figures who opposed the regime. This included the rock group Plastic People of the Universe, whose members were arrested on such spurious grounds as having long hair.

Throughout his life, Havel continued to write, including an essay titled *The Power of the*

Powerless. That work included his most famous words, "live within a lie," summing up the everyday experience of many ordinary people. Havel correctly surmised that after 1968, many Czechoslovaks had retreated behind cynicism and despair while still rejecting the legitimacy of the regime.

Havel

Havel's most notable early political achievement was his co-authorship of Charter 77, a group of dissidents who challenged the communist authorities in 1977. Charter 77 emerged as a response both to the crushing of the Prague Spring and the thaw in the geopolitical environment. Understandably, there was widespread despair in Czechoslovakia after the Soviet invasion of August 1968 and the subsequent removal of Dubček from power, and major crackdown took place in the aftermath, imprisoning dissidents, banning Prague Spring-linked organisations, and "blacklisting" particularly outspoken individuals (or at least those whom the authorities deemed a threat).

The period that followed was called "Normalization" and overseen by the new, pliant communist leader, Gustáv Husák. Despite that name, however, this era was simply a period of grudging, bitter acceptance, as many of the protestors from 1968 simply went underground, biding their time and influencing society outside the corridors of authority.[83] Despite the best efforts of the secret police, dissident activity could not be completely stamped out, and throughout the 1970s, tensions bubbled under the surface of Czechoslovak society.

Meanwhile, the geopolitical environment was shifting. Although they were not fully aware of the other's difficulties, both the Soviet Union and the United States were experiencing tumult by the end of the 1960s. The Soviets were battling with the Chinese for primacy within the communist world and had almost come to blows with their giant neighbour. Moreover, the arms race was proving ruinously expensive, and Russia's stuttering economy, which would only worsen in the 1970s, was unable to pay for this huge budget. The Soviets, in short, wanted to find a way to reduce arms spending without conceding much in political terms to the West.

The United States, meanwhile, had been drawn into the terribly expensive Vietnam War, which corroded the legitimacy of the ruling classes and led to political unrest at home. Some observers wondered if the country was becoming ungovernable in the 1960s, and its leaders were desperate to reduce military spending and leave Vietnam without losing too much face in the process.

The outcome of these two approaches was known as détente, or "relaxation," and it would prove crucial for the burgeoning Czechoslovak underground movement when the communist regime fell. Détente manifested itself in a number of ways, most notably arms limitation agreements and other international treaties brokered by an unlikely combination of conservative American politicians, such as Richard Nixon, Gerald Ford, and Henry Kissinger, and the Soviet gerontocracy led by Leonid Brezhnev. The nuclear Non-Proliferation Treaty (NPT), Anti-Ballistic Missile Treaty (ABM) and Strategic Arms Limitation Talks all managed to reduce tension between the two sides in the late 1960s and early 1970s, at least for a time. The last part of the détente process was the 1975 Helsinki Final Act, signed by all the European countries and their superpower sponsors.[84] The Helsinki Final Act was an attractive proposition for the communist countries because it recognised the post-1945 borders of Europe, some of which were previously disputed by the West, including the partition of Germany. The Helsinki process appeared to have permanently partitioned the continent into two blocs and left the Czechs and the Slovaks behind the Iron Curtain.

[83] Gerald Knaus, "Europe and Azerbaijan: The End of Shame", *Journal of Democracy,* (2015, pp. 5-18)
[84] Gerald Knaus, "Europe and Azerbaijan: The End of Shame", *Journal of Democracy,* (2015, pp. 5-18)

In the process however, the Helsinki Final Act included a provision for a permanent institution in Europe, the Commission on Security and Cooperation in Europe (CSCE), which was a product of the so-called "Third Basket" of the Helsinki Accords. This basket included certain assurances regarding human rights, which may seem odd given that authoritarian regimes trampled those rights each day, including in Czechoslovakia. It seems the communist regimes thought that human rights commitments were superficial and impossible to enforce, so as long as they achieved the objective they really wanted (border recognition), they would pay lip service to liberal values like human rights and the body set up to report on them, the CSCE.

This turned out to be a fatal miscalculation, nowhere more so than in Czechoslovakia. Not long after the Helsinki process began in 1975, the dissidents who had cut their teeth during the Prague Spring would launch their direct challenge against the Czechoslovak authorities, and the rebels would directly cite the Helsinki commitments. On January 6, 1977, a manifesto was leaked to a number of West German newspapers called Charter 77, signed by 243 prominent Czechoslovak artists, dissidents, and even some officials, calling for the regime to honor the commitments made under the Helsinki Final Act and the CSCE.[85] Human rights, significantly, were cited as a major theme.[86]

This group included Havel and a number of other well-known dissidents, such as Jiří Němec, Václav Benda, Ladislav Hejdánek, and Jan Patočka. The Charter was motivated by the arrest of a progressive rock band, Plastic People of the Universe, the previous year. Indeed, political prisoners would be a key concern of the groups that emerged after the Helsinki Final Act was signed.

Charter 77 was distributed amongst the prominent Western publications, including the *New York Times* and radio stations such as Radio Free Europe. For the United States, it was a huge propaganda gift, which was ironic considering the Americans had opposed the insertion of Human Rights provisions into the Helsinki Final Act. As it turned out, the human rights commitments would now prove to be a crucial tool of soft power in the Cold War, which was about to enter another acute phase after the Soviets invaded Afghanistan in December 1979 and Ronald Reagan won the presidency in 1980.

In the late 1970s in Czechoslovakia, the signs did not look as good as hindsight suggests. Czech and Slovak nationalism had been thoroughly repressed by the communist authorities, and the liberals, after the publication of Charter 77, were now underground or being monitored. In fact, many of the Charter 77 signatories were hounded by the Husák regime, and while some fled the country and went into exile, others were imprisoned and interrogated, sometimes for years. Havel, for instance, was imprisoned on several occasions, including one stint of four years

---

[85] Emily Tamkin, "In Charter 77, Czech Dissidents Charted New Territory", *Foreign Policy*, 3 February 2017, https://foreignpolicy.com/2017/02/03/in-charter-77-czech-dissidents-charted-new-territory/, [accessed 10 April 2019]

[86] Gerald Knaus, "Europe and Azerbaijan: The End of Shame", *Journal of Democracy,* (2015, pp. 5-18)

between 1979-1983.[87] As for the band so feared by the regime, Plastic People of the Universe, they were harassed by the authorities, intermittently imprisoned, and some of the group emigrated to Canada. They would not perform in Czechoslovakia openly again – they returned to the Czech Republic to perform in 1997 for a 20th anniversary show to commemorate Charter 77.

As the 1980s dawned, the prospect of change in Czechoslovakia looked bleak. The 1968 Prague Spring may have excited reformers, and Charter 77 indicated a shifting continental stance on Human Rights, but for all intents and purposes the entire communist bloc looked stuck in a phase of stagnation in the 1980s. The Husák administration was an orthodox communist regime, consisting of elderly, grey, and essentially conservative leaders, and Central and Eastern European communists trotted out the same old slogans and party jargon, brushing the bad news under the carpet, denouncing the West wherever possible, and making laughably false claims about their own economic prowess. The Czechoslovaks had traditionally been more Western-facing in their outlook, but in the 1980s, Czechoslovakia was not particularly different from its peers. Over time, Hungary ploughed a more economically-liberal furrow, and Poland seemed more influenced by religious and nationalist feeling. East Germany and Romania were particularly repressive, but Yugoslavia trod its own autonomous path, experiencing more prosperity in the process. Czechoslovakia had even less distinguishing elements.

The advent of Mikhail Gorbachev's rule in the Soviet Union was in many ways a revival of the "socialism with a human face" ideas that emanated during the Prague Spring two decades before. In addition, Gorbachev had the power to roll back the Soviet military presence hanging over Central and Eastern Europe, essentially ending the Brezhnev Doctrine, which had essentially promised Soviet intervention should a client state drift too far from Moscow's line.

Like many regimes in the communist bloc, the Soviet Union was bereft of new ideas and made up of orthodox communists, most of whom were very old men. Embarrassingly, the Soviet Union had lost three geriatric leaders in the space of three years from 1982-1985,[88] so the ruling Politburo turned to an up and coming reform-minded and relatively youthful new leader after the death of Konstantin Chernenko in 1985. Aware that the communist system was in dire straits, Gorbachev, who was in his 50s, embarked upon a breathtaking reform agenda. Realizing that the Soviet command economy structure was totally inadequate to meet the needs of the country's people and its military ambitions, Gorbachev attempted to revive the energies of the population, and he believed a more open society might be the answer to the USSR's stagnation, setting about first *Glasnost* then *Perestroika*, translating as "openness" and "restructuring." These reforms blew away the inertia endemic in Soviet culture, and suddenly, it felt like everything was changing. Criticism was suddenly permitted, and many censures were removed. Gorbachev

---

[87] Emily Tamkin, "In Charter 77, Czech Dissidents Charted New Territory", *Foreign Policy*, 3 February 2017, https://foreignpolicy.com/2017/02/03/in-charter-77-czech-dissidents-charted-new-territory/, [accessed 10 April 2019]

[88] Godfrey Hodgson, *People's Century: From the dawn of the century to the eve of the millennium* (Godalming: BBC Books, 1998)

became a celebrity in the West and simultaneously gave hope to people in the wider communist bloc, even as he terrified its leaders.[89]

At the same time he implemented these liberalizing reforms, Gorbachev knew that the Soviet Union could not sustain its level of military spending, especially after President Reagan unveiled his so-called "Star Wars" program, the Strategic Defence Initiative (SDI). As a result, the Soviet leader sought ways to reduce his country's military costs by ending the war in Afghanistan, signing arms control agreements with the United States, and, crucially for Czechoslovakia, reducing its military presence in Central and Eastern Europe.

Although the country was home to some of the best-known anti-communist dissidents of the era, Gorbachev was actually concerned by the slow pace of reform in Czechoslovakia in the late 1980s. This, of course, could be one of the reasons a revolution eventually swept the country, and it was clear that Gorbachev believed a *Glasnost* style opening could head off an insurrection. This point remains highly contested by historians, but dissent certainly started to show itself, after 20 years of repression, at the beginning of 1988.

The communist leader, Gustáv Husák, was typical of the region's old-fashioned hardliners. He had no interest in the kind of reform on show in the USSR, but eventually, under pressure internally and externally, he yielded to at least the semblance of a reform package in April 1987. Later that year he gave way and stood down as General Secretary of the Communist Party in favor of Miloš Jakeš, who was considered somewhat more progressive. Husák remained on the ruling Politburo until the regime's demise at the end of 1989.

Jakeš, 10 years Husák's junior but still by this point 65 years old, appeared to support Gorbachev's vision of a reformed communist system, but he proved timid in how far he was willing to go. He would quickly be tested by demonstrations and showed little appetite in entering into a dialogue in the manner of the authorities in Poland.

The first major demonstration to take place in the new, slightly more open atmosphere came on March 25, 1988 in Bratislava, today the capital of Slovakia. The so-called "Candle" demonstration, organised by activists Marián Šťastný and František Mikloško, was the most significant protest of its kind to take place since the Soviet invasion of 1968. Although the numbers are disputed, several thousand started a candlelit vigil protesting against the authority's suppression of religious liberty. Walking towards the city's main square holding candles, the demonstrators were very much in the mold of the Solidarity movement in Poland. Primarily religious in their motives, the Candle demonstrators were not only venting the frustration of many in the Catholic country, but also hitting one of the regime's vulnerabilities, because they were very reluctant to appear to be actively against the church. Nevertheless, this did not prevent a crackdown on the protestors with the use of batons and water cannons.

---

[89] Ibid.

The people had challenged the regime, testing whether it was open to talks or real reform, and the authorities had fallen back on tried and tested methods of repression. It would not be sufficient, however, to dampen growing sentiment that the country needed to change.

The events in Bratislava and the Candle demonstrators led to the organisztion of a larger protest on August 21, 1988. The date was heavy with symbolism, as it marked 20 years since the Soviet invasion that crushed the Prague Spring. This time, the organizers were overtly political, and the protests were called by Charter 77, which was now recognized as a human rights organization. Charter 77 and affiliated groups which would ultimately come under the umbrella of the Civic Forum.[90]

The communist authorities were wary of the protestors and urged them, in vain, not to attend the rally. 10,000 people attended the demonstration, calling for political reform, greater freedom, and the departure of the 80,000 Soviet troops stationed in the country.[91] Predictably, the regime cracked down on the demonstrators, using tear gas and batons as they arrested dozens of people. More dissidents were later rounded up by the authorities and their ubiquitous secret police.[92]

This did little to deter dissenters, however. Perhaps sensing the fraying of the dictatorship, another demonstration was called for on October 28, 1988 in Prague and other cities across the country, this time to mark the 70th anniversary of the founding of Czechoslovakia. The protests followed a similar pattern to those that came before, as thousands came out into the streets and were met by heavy-handed police tactics and then arrests. The scenes were also witnessed by Western journalists who eagerly reported events to the foreign press.

It wouldn't be long until one of the key demands of the dissidents was met. In December 1988, Mikhail Gorbachev gave a speech to the United Nations General Assembly that would hasten the end of the Cold War and the role of communism in Czechoslovakia. In his speech, Gorbachev announced military cuts and troop withdrawals - in essence, the Soviet leader was withdrawing the Soviet military umbrella from Central and Eastern Europe.[93] The Warsaw Pact might have still been in existence, but without the explicit backing of the USSR, it would lose its credibility. When it was suggested that the Soviet Union's satellite states might break out of Moscow's orbit, Gorbachev apparently seemed willing to let the states choose their path, or "go their own way,"

---

[90] *The New York Times,* "Police Attack Protesters at Prague Demonstration", 29 October 1988, https://www.nytimes.com/1988/10/29/world/police-attack-protesters-at-prague-demonstration.html, [accessed 10 April 2019]

[91] *The New York Times,* "Police Attack Protesters at Prague Demonstration", 29 October 1988, https://www.nytimes.com/1988/10/29/world/police-attack-protesters-at-prague-demonstration.html, [accessed 2 April 2019]

[92] *The New York Times,* "Police Attack Protesters at Prague Demonstration", 29 October 1988, https://www.nytimes.com/1988/10/29/world/police-attack-protesters-at-prague-demonstration.html, [accessed 2 April 2019]

[93] *The New York Times,* "The Gorbachev Visit; Excerpts From Speech to U.N. on Major Soviet Military Cuts", 8 December 1988, https://www.nytimes.com/1988/12/08/world/the-gorbachev-visit-excerpts-from-speech-to-un-on-major-soviet-military-cuts.html [accessed 2 April 2019]

which came to be known as the "Sinatra Doctrine."

The significance for Czechoslovakia of Gorbachev's announcement was huge. For the regime, it opened up the possibility that without the Soviet military stationed in the country, it might not be able to withstand an insurrection. For the dissidents, on the other hand, the threat of a Soviet occupation appeared to have receded, the very thing that had engendered so much despair in the intervening 20 years.

The withdrawal of the Soviet military from Czechoslovakia had other profound implications. Czechoslovak leaders had been consistently concerned about the state's geopolitical security for as long as the nation existed, due to its position in the center of Europe. If the country really had the option to break out of the Warsaw Pact, would its people choose domestic communism? And if not, would it look to the East, West, or a more independent path?

Few thought that 1989 would be revolutionary as the year itself dawned, but the pressures that would topple authoritarian regimes were already on the move, including in Czechoslovakia. The biggest anti-government protest to date occurred on January 16, 1989, marking the 20th anniversary of the self-immolation of student Jan Palach. To demonstrate against the Soviet occupying forces in 1969, the 20-year-old Palach set himself on fire in Prague's Wenceslas Square, and his memory had a galvanizing impact on those who took to the streets in 1989. Like in previous protests, the crowds were dispersed by the security forces, but dissidents remained committed to civil disobedience.

The regime flailed in an increasingly desperate manner to contain the protests, and in February that year it turned to its favorite repressive mechanism: imprisoning Havel. Convicted for inciting the illegal protests and obstructing the police, Havel was jailed for nine months.[94] It was the playwright's third prison sentence and also his last.

Persecuting Havel was deeply counterproductive for the regime, only increasing the influence of the dissident and reinforcing its own moral bankruptcy. Havel made a statement outlining this stance after his sentencing: "I do not feel guilty, but if sentenced, I will accept the punishment as a sacrifice for a good cause, which is nothing in the face of the ultimate sacrifice of Jan Palach, which we sought to commemorate."[95] The Havel verdict also led to criticism from Western Europeans, who argued the 1975 Helsinki Final Act should be protecting the activities of Charter 77.[96]

---

[94] John Tagliabue, Prague Jails a Major Playwright For Inciting Protests Last Month, *The New York Times*, 22 February 1989, https://www.nytimes.com/1989/02/22/world/prague-jails-a-major-playwright-for-inciting-protests-last-month.html, [accessed 3 April 2019]

[95] John Tagliabue, Prague Jails a Major Playwright For Inciting Protests Last Month, *The New York Times*, 22 February 1989, https://www.nytimes.com/1989/02/22/world/prague-jails-a-major-playwright-for-inciting-protests-last-month.html, [accessed 3 April 2019]

[96] John Tagliabue, Prague Jails a Major Playwright For Inciting Protests Last Month, *The New York Times*, 22 February 1989, https://www.nytimes.com/1989/02/22/world/prague-jails-a-major-playwright-for-inciting-

Václav Havel served half of his sentence before being released on May 18, 1989 after protests calling for his freedom and after Czechoslovakia had signed a treaty in Vienna once again reinforcing its commitment to human rights.[97] It was clear the communist authorities were increasingly trapping themselves; willing to use force, but not enough to deter protests, the regime felt obliged to superficially support individual rights initiatives, clearly revealing its own hypocrisy while offering some hope to the country's benighted citizens. The situation could not persist.

Many accounts of the end of communism in 1989 start with the fall of the Berlin Wall on November 9 of that year, but in many ways the East Germans were a little late to the party. In Poland, the communist government had convened the so-called "Round Table" talks at the start of the year and held the first democratic elections in the communist world since the 1940s. Unsurprisingly, non-communist politicians won the June 1989 polls, and the Polish regime abided by the result and agreed to a transition to a civilian, democratic leadership. Similarly, in Hungary, economic liberal reforms had occurred over the course of the 1980s and ultimately led to some political relaxation. In the summer of 1989, the Hungarians effectively opened the border with Austria, or at least they did not enforce it with the same rigor expected of a Warsaw Pact state. This opened the floodgates for East German citizens, who then used the route to travel to West Germany. It was common for people to holiday in other communist countries, and that summer many East Germans were spending their vacation in Hungary. Seeing that the border with Austria appeared to be unguarded, a number of East Germans attempted to cross the frontier in August 1989, and they were unimpeded. 900 then tried and succeeded in making it over the border.[98] Suddenly, East Germans saw their chance and thousands attempted to make the journey to freedom.

With the borders now apparently permeable, the entire region found itself in a state of flux. What is sometimes lost in the retelling of this heady period was that for many of the weeks and months before the fall of the Berlin Wall, the emphasis was on East German refugees attempting to flee to the West. The refugees sought escape routes in various West German embassies in other communist countries, which increased when the East German authorities attempted to close its own borders and stop its people making it to the West. One of the locations most famously involved was the West German embassy in Prague. East Germans were trying to claim asylum at the embassy, and this was actively encouraged by the Bonn government in West Germany. They were even offered cash incentives for making it to West Germany. After a period of diplomatic tension, the West Germans were granted safe passage out of the Prague Embassy and to the Federal Republic. Europe had not seen such desperate migration since before the building of the

protests-last-month.html, [accessed 3 April 2019]

[97] John Tagliabue, "Czech Playwright Released From Prison", *The New York Times*, 18 May 1989, https://www.nytimes.com/1989/05/18/world/czech-playwright-freed-from-prison.html, [accessed 3 April 2019]

[98] W. Mayr, 'Hungary's Peaceful Revolution Cutting the Fence and Changing History', *Der Spiegel*, 29 May 2009, http://www.spiegel.de/international/europe/hungary-s-peaceful-revolution-cutting-the-fence-and-changing-history-a-627632.html, [accessed 31 January 2019]

Berlin Wall in 1961.[99]

Meanwhile, Mikhail Gorbachev was desperately urging communist leaders to reform and allow more political openness. At this time, the Czechoslovaks were not at the forefront of the revolt that was sweeping the continent, but they would soon make their mark with their own Velvet Revolution.

By October 1989, Erich Honecker had been forced to step down in East Germany, Poland had already held elections, Hungary was opening up its economy and *Glasnost*-led political upheaval was beginning to create turmoil in Gorbachev's Soviet Union. On October 28, demonstrations swept across Czechoslovakia, a sign that protestors were frustrated at the slow response of the authorities in their country compared to neighbors such as Poland. Wenceslas Square was the epicenter of the protests, a huge meeting point in the center of Prague, and it was to become synonymous with the end of communism in the entire region. First, though, the events in Berlin would act as a catalyst for a more widespread uprising.[100]

The East German government was rocking by November 1989. Pressure was mounting for the regime to open its border positions, at least to other communist countries so East Germans could make the long journey to the West. Finally, this happened and effectively the Berlin Wall's reason for being was ceasing to exist. More protests followed in various East German cities, and after a confused announcement regarding travel to West Berlin, thousands gathered near the Berlin Wall on the night of November 9, 1989. Things could have turned out very differently if the border guards had tried to prevent East Berliners crossing the frontier that night, but they stood down and East Germans streamed over into the western side of the city. There were wild scenes of celebration as East Berliners and West Berliners celebrated their apparent reunification. East Germany would only survive another 11 months, and Germany was reunified on October 3, 1990.

Meanwhile, people across the communist world saw the fall of the Berlin Wall as their opportunity. They noted that the Soviets had not intervened or threatened to intervene, which meant Gorbachev's declaration to pull out Soviet forces from Central and Eastern Europe the previous November seemed to be legitimate. Moreover, the internal security forces had not tried to suppress the crowds, which would have been a near certainty in the years before 1989. Citizens living across the region knew if these two elements held true in their own countries, they too could overthrow their own hated regimes.

---

[99] Norman M. Naimark, *The Russians in Germany: A History of the Soviet Zone of Occupation, 1945-1949* (Harvard: Harvard University Press, 1995), pp. 132, 133, Ferdinand Protzman, 'Jubilant East Germans Cross to West in Sealed Trains', *New York Times*, 6 October 1989, http://www.nytimes.com/1989/10/06/world/jubilant-east-germans-cross-to-west-in-sealed-trains.html, [accessed 28 January 2019]

[100] Godfrey Hodgson, *People's Century: From the dawn of the century to the eve of the millennium* (Godalming: BBC Books, 1998)

Events moved quickly in Czechoslovakia. A week after the fall of the Berlin Wall, on November 16, students organized a peaceful demonstration in Bratislava. Václav Havel organized demonstrations in Prague for the following day, which were broken up by the police.[101] Strikes, initially focused around theaters, then enveloped the country, and the ruling Politburo began to seriously worry about the direction in which events were heading. The first meeting of the Civic Forum with Prime Minister Ladislav Adamec took place on November 21, despite the fact the Civic Forum had only been formed days beforehand as a front organization for the likes of Havel's Charter 77 movement and the Slovak group Public Against Violence.

Mass demonstrations began on November 22 in Bratislava, and then a general strike began. The protestors could sense that the regime was teetering, and on November 24, Jakeš stood down as General Secretary and was replaced by the more moderate Karel Urbánek. The Civic Forum was in no mood to accommodate the communists in any transition of power, and their role in public life was officially removed from the constitution on November 29. An interim government, including some non-communists, took office on December 10, and Havel became president on December 29, the culmination of a heady few weeks in the country. Other countries in the region followed, with the exception of Romania, where Ceausescu was violently overthrown and executed.

Yugoslavia's Dissolution

Yugoslavia had straddled the line between economic frailty and independent prosperity throughout its history. Tito had managed to secure loans and financial aid from the West while retaining close relations - and therefore trade - with the communist bloc. Indeed, Yugoslavia was a rare example of a country that traded with both east and west. As a result, GDP per capita was higher in Yugoslavia than many of its contemporaries in Central Europe and Eastern Europe.

The Yugoslav model was seen by many as an acceptable socialist system, particularly considering its arrangement of local worker control over factories and production, but by the end of the 1980s, it was suffering from similar problems facing other communist countries. This was due to a combination of the world recession in the early 1980s and resulting high interest rates (and related hikes in interest payments and debt), as well as chronically low productivity, high unemployment, and emigration to other European countries.[102] In the late 1980s Yugoslavia went into a severe recession, made worse by mounting levels of debt. The IMF was called in to provide an emergency loan, and Yugoslavia had already received debt relief in 1983 and 1984, a particularly acute point in its crisis after a campaign by the American-led group "Friends of Yugoslavia."[103]

---

[101] BBC News, "1989: Police crush Prague protest rally", http://news.bbc.co.uk/onthisday/hi/dates/stories/november/17/newsid_2540000/2540171.stm, [accessed 7 April 2019]

[102] Ann Lane, *Yugoslavia: When Ideals Collide*, (Basingstoke: Palgrave Macmillan, 2004), p. 158.

[103] John R. Lampe, *Yugoslavia as History. Twice there was a country.* (Cambridge: Cambridge University Press,

The Cold War came to a sudden climax in 1989 when the Berlin Wall fell, and the special geopolitical position of Yugoslavia was now redundant. American political scientist Francis Fukuyama famously declared that this marked the "End of History,"[104] and that the world was now moving into a period of universal liberal democracy and market capitalism. "Washington Consensus" was coined to describe the pro-market policies pursued by the likes of the IMF and World Bank. When the Soviet Union dissolved formally in 1991, the West had seemingly triumphed in its confrontation against communism, and there would be no room for even hybrid models such as Yugoslavia's. Indeed, Yugoslavia was quickly put into this new paradigm, at least in the economic sphere. As with so many other examples during the period, a sclerotic, low growth and low productivity economy was prescribed a tough dose of austerity and liberalization in return for emergency financial assistance.

The role this "structural adjustment" program played in the onset of violence in Yugoslavia has been disputed. Some believe that it simply increased unhappiness about the status quo and heralded a more rapid disintegration of the Federation. Others believed that the IMF package was the last opportunity Yugoslavia had to reform.

The man in charge of its implementation was Ante Marković. Marković was a Bosnian Croat who had fought with Tito's Partisans during the Second World War. A communist, Marković had been President of Croatia from 1986-1988, and he became Yugoslav Prime Minister in March 1989. It is perhaps ironic then that Marković would be entrusted with implementing this most capitalist set of policies.

Despite his background, Marković was an enthusiastic economic reformer, believing the IMF package was necessary.[105] Marković tied the currency (the Dinar) to the German Mark, attempting state privatization and trade liberalization.[106] Although the initial results were uneven, Marković's reforms did appear to curb inflation and improve incomes. He was also popular and one of the last prominent pan-Yugoslav politicians of any heft. Marković was sharply critical of the leaders who had swerved towards nationalism, including Milošević, as well as Borisav Jović in Serbia and Radovan Karadžić in Bosnia and Herzegovina. Marković was both a man of the future and the past, committed not only to economic reform and a better standard of living for Yugoslavs but also rooted in the socialist view of the country as a fraternal enterprise. He was, however, unsuited to the atmosphere of Yugoslavia in its final phase, a time in which most nominally communist politicians had retreated behind nationalist shields. He desperately tried to curtail the descent into conflict in 1990 and 1991, but the politicians around him had already drawn the battle lines.

2000), pp. 322-323.

[104] Francis Fukuyama, 'The End of History?', *The National Interest*, No. 16 (Summer 1989), pp. 3-18.

[105] John R. Lampe, *Yugoslavia as History. Twice there was a country.* (Cambridge: Cambridge University Press, 2000), pp. 352-355.

[106] Carole Rogel, *The Breakup of Yugoslavia and its Aftermath* (London: Greenwood Press, 2004), p. 21.

Marković

The most visible moment before conflicts engulfed Yugoslavia was the 1990 Communist Party Congress, officially termed the 14th Congress of the League of Communists of Yugoslavia, which took place in Belgrade in late January 1990. The congress was called as an extraordinary meeting to discuss the various political disputes that had arisen since the previous meeting in 1986. With the Cold War quickly winding down, the different parties reverted to previous inclinations at the congress. The main dispute was between the Serbian and Slovenian delegations over the former's centralization proposals, whereas the latter wanted more autonomy for the republics. The Serbs made a number of proposals for which they could now achieve majority decisions. Milošević's manoeuvring since 1987 meant that he had, essentially, appointees and allies in charge of the Kosovo, Vojvodina, and Montenegro delegations, as well as his own Serb party. This meant Milošević commanded a bloc vote that could pass or strike down any decision he chose.

The congress dragged on for two days, full of arguments, rows, and disagreements. Milan Kučan told the Serb delegation that he needed at least the appearance of compromise over his suggestions. When this proved not to be forthcoming, the Slovenian delegation resigned and stormed out of the convention hall. Initially, the Croats were unsure of what to do and Milošević tried to persuade them to remain, knowing he could still maintain the semblance of unity even without the Slovenes. Nevertheless, after some deliberation, the Croats joined the Slovenes by leaving. The delegations from Macedonia and Bosnia and Herzegovina followed.

Whether this was all by Milošević's design or an unintended effect of his aggressive actions is hard to discern, but either way, the League was now dead.[107] The country itself was now in serious peril, decoupled as it was from the socialist ideology that had bound it together for 45

---

[107] Carole Rogel, *The Breakup of Yugoslavia and its Aftermath* (London: Greenwood Press, 2004), pp. 18-19.

years. Socialist ideology was giving way to the nationalist variety, and this movement clearly pointed to self-determination and democracy in other communist countries. The end of the Cold War and the winds of change that swept through the continent would prove more problematic in Yugoslavia, a country with so many sectarian identities.

Yugoslavia limped on throughout 1990. Without the League, the Federation was exposed even more to nationalist unrest. It was not possible for every republic to simply split from the Federation, however. Slovenia may have been mostly Slovene, but there was a significant minority of Serbs in Croatia and Kosovo. Ethnic Albanians made up a sizeable minority in Macedonia, while Bosnia and Herzegovina were almost equally divided three ways between the majority Bosnian Muslims (or Bosniaks), Bosnian Serbs, and Bosnian Croats. Independence into nationalist states unnerved the minorities, which then looked towards their majority republic for protection. This then led to ideas of Greater Croatia and Greater Serbia, which implied some territorial conquest. The number of people who identified as "Yugoslav," as opposed to their individual nationalities, was in steep decline, and only significant in number in the most ethnically-mixed republic, Bosnia and Herzegovina.[108]

Despite the issues, some political reforms took place in the country's final days. Elections were held on April 8, 1990 in each republic, the first since the 1940s. Nationalists and independence-minded parties swept the elections. Franjo Tudjman's hard-line Croatian Democratic Union (HDZ) party won in Croatia by promising to "defend" the republic from Milošević. This led to Belgrade endorsing resistance to the HDZ, or as Belgrade put it, the NDH. Croatian Serbs in Knin, in the Krajina area, led by police inspector Milan Martić, formed a militia and seized control of the region. A sizeable section of Croatia was now effectively outside the control of Tudjman's government in Zagreb. The Serb-dominated Yugoslav National Army (JNA), meanwhile, was guaranteeing the security of Serb minorities outside Serbia.

In late 1990 and early 1991 conflict had essentially begun in Krajina and was looming elsewhere in the Federation. Ante Marković was desperately trying to stabilise Yugoslavia's economy, even as his country would soon start losing its component parts.

The first to leave was Slovenia, which was never considered the most problematic of Yugoslavia's republics. One of the three key founder members in 1918 as part of the Kingdom of Serbs, Croats and Slovenes, the crucial confrontations had consistently been between Serbia and Croatia, whereas Slovenes saw themselves as more "European" than the other more "Balkan" republics. Slovenia had been part of the Austro-Hungarian Empire and therefore more a part of "civilized" Central Europe. It was also the only Catholic region in Yugoslavia besides Croatia. Slovenia's language was also different than the other republics, where Serbo-Croat dominated. Many young people in 1980s Slovenia had been behind the push towards greater democratic

---

[108] Vesna Drapac, *Constructing Yugoslavia: A Transnational History*, (Basingstoke: Palgrave Macmillan, 2010), p. 248.

accountability, and Slovene President Milan Kučan had exploited the tension in Kosovo to promote greater autonomy set apart from central (Serb) domination.

After leading the walkout of the January 1990 congress, it seemed only a matter of time before Slovenia withdrew further support from Belgrade.[109] As the rest of Europe attempted to cope with the challenges presented by the fall of the Berlin Wall, Slovenia prepared to hold a referendum on continuing membership in the Yugoslav Federation. On December 23, Slovenia held its referendum, during which 88% of voters opted for independence.

Distracted by events elsewhere in Yugoslavia, Belgrade was slow to respond. Although this did not energize nationalists in the same way it would've if Bosnia and Herzegovina or Kosovo had declared an intention to break away, the Slovene decision was actually the death knell for Yugoslavia. If it was allowed to leave unimpeded, it would surely only be a matter of time before Croatia declared independence. It was a precedent that contained its own logic.

Six months later, on June 25, 1991, Slovenia declared formal independence, and in response, the Yugoslav authorities dispatched the JNA to prevent the Slovene breakaway. Slovenia had few troops or military equipment, save the Slovene sections of the federal army, called the Slovenian Territorial Defence (TO). In a straight fight between the JNA and the Slovene forces, it would have been no contest.

A number of issues ensured that the so-called "Ten Day War" was by far the least destructive of the conflicts that gripped Yugoslavia throughout the 1990s. Most importantly, the JNA relied on the Serbs, who had to travel through Croatia and who were by no means supportive of the action. The soldiers had little incentive to fight, with the ethnicity issue neutralized in the case of Slovenia. Furthermore, there was no official force as such to fight; the TO had been organized into guerrilla fighting units, ready to engage in asymmetric warfare with 21,000 personnel.

On June 26, 1991 the Yugoslav army moved into Slovenia and came into contact with TO militias.[110] Slovene politicians immediately attempted to garner international support for their independence, and against the Yugoslav army's actions. The United Nations called for an end to the fighting, with this pressure bearing almost immediate fruit. The Yugoslavs were persuaded to come to the negotiating table, and a ceasefire was announced on July 2. Five days later, an agreement was signed on the island of Brioni, incidentally one of Tito's favorite residences, to bring the fighting to an official end. The "Brioni Accord" recognized Slovene independence and ended the short war. During the fighting, 44 Yugoslav soldiers and 18 Slovene TO troops had been killed. These casualty figures would be dwarfed by the later Balkan wars, a sign that other nationalist leaders may have thought that leaving Yugoslavia would be relatively straightforward

---

[109] Carole Rogel, *The Breakup of Yugoslavia and its Aftermath* (London: Greenwood Press, 2004), pp. 18-19.

[110] John Tagliabue, 'Yugoslav Army Uses Force in Breakaway Republic; Slovenia Reports 100 Wounded or Killed', *The New York Times*, 28 June 1991, https://www.nytimes.com/1991/06/28/world/yugoslav-army-uses-force-breakaway-republic-slovenia-reports-100-wounded-killed.html, [accessed 31 October 1991]

after Slovenia.

Slovene independence was not immediately recognized by the international community, which was unsure of how to respond to nationalist agitation in Yugoslavia. It would be another six months, in January 1992 when Slovene independence was widely recognized and almost a year until it was accepted as a member of the United Nations. By this point, conflict was raging across the Federation, firstly in Croatia and then in Bosnia and Herzegovina.

The Croats had generally sided with the Slovenes as internecine politics emerged in the late 1980s. With Ljubljana exiting Yugoslavia in 1990-1991, it was clear that many Croat nationalists would also want independence. Franjo Tudjman had positioned himself as the leader of the separatists by this time, and his HDZ party had already won an electoral victory in 1990.

Croatia, however, was a far more complex issue. The main point of tension throughout Yugoslavia's history had in fact been between Serbs and Croats. This had manifested itself in the 1920s, when a Serb had assassinated the popular Croat politician Stjepan Radić. The Ustaše leader Ante Pavelić successfully plotted to murder Yugoslav King Alexander in 1934, and during the Second World War, the Nazi-backed Croat state, the NDH regime, had terrorized other Yugoslav nationalities, most significantly the Serbs. The animosity had remerged during the Croatian Spring unrest in the 1960s and 1970s. As central authority broke down in the Yugoslav Federation in the late 1980s, therefore, it did not take long for suspicion to increase between Serbs and Croats.

Separation would be difficult for Tudjman and his allies. First, Croatia contained a large Serb minority, and some Serbs had already taken matters into their own hands during the uprising in Knin in Krajina in 1990. Belgrade feared, correctly, that Croat troops would attempt to retake the enclave by force, while the Croats worried that Milošević was developing a Greater Serbia project. The Serbian strongman had by now fashioned a reputation as a defender of the Serbs, and he seemed unlikely to allow such a large number of Serbs to break away into a separate state that was potentially hostile to their interests.[111] Unlike in Slovenia, any political move would likely trigger a military response from the JNA, which by now was the only arbiter of order within the Federation. This was problematic since it was increasingly seen as a Serb-dominated army.[112]

Tension rose in early 1991 when the "Špegelj Tapes" were uncovered by Yugoslav media. They appeared to record the Croatian Defence Minister, Martin Špegelj, arranging the shipment of arms to Croat depots via Hungary. The revelation heightened fears that Croatia was about to break away from the rest of the Federation. An independence referendum was then held on May

[111] Tom Buchanan, *Europe's Troubled Peace. 1945 to the Present* (Chichester: Wiley-Blackwell, 2012, 2nd ed), p. 242.

[112] John R. Lampe, *Yugoslavia as History. Twice there was a country* (Cambridge: Cambridge University Press, 2000), p. 332.

2, 1991, with 93% of voters opting for autonomy. Tudjman subsequently declared independence on June 25, the same day as the Slovenes.

While Slovenia successfully left after a short war, Croatia would face a much tougher departure. In fact, Croatia would be at war for over four years. Milošević's argument to the Croats was that the principle of self-determination should apply to Serbs in the country, therefore giving them the option to separate from the rest of Croatia. This was obviously anathema to the Croat leadership.

There were some large regions of majority-Serb populations. One was the Krajina, which included Knin and bordered Serb-dominated parts of Bosnia and Herzegovina. The others were Western Slavonia and Eastern Slavonia, in the northeast of Croatia and bordering Serbia. All three areas were backed by Serbia, supplied with weapons and diplomatic support. They soon declared themselves autonomous regions, outside the sovereignty of any Croat state.

Fighting had broken out between Serbs and Croats in Plitvice in April 1991, an area of conjoining lakes popular among tourists, but this low-level conflict expanded into a full-scale war. Nominally protecting Serbs in the autonomous regions, the JNA moved on the major coastal Croatian cities of Split and Dubrovnik in the summer of 1991 after the independence declaration.[113] By shelling these cities indiscriminately, the JNA was besieging the Croats and terrorizing their populations, attempting to extort political concessions from Zagreb. At the time, the JNA claimed it was targeting Ustaše terrorists in both cities.

Following this initial reasoning, the Serbs and their allies the Montenegrins set their sights on capturing the ancient city of Dubrovnik. Both Split and Dubrovnik were hugely popular with Western tourists. The latter was dubbed the "Pearl of the Adriatic," and therefore a significant source of foreign currency for Croatia. The sieges hit the fledgling Croatian state financially and in terms of prestige, and the fighting caused cultural vandalism in the process. This latter point was probably important in the swift international condemnation that was aimed at Belgrade and the Yugoslav leadership from the international community.

Shortly after Slovenia and Croatia declared independence in June 1991 and fighting erupted, the United Nations and European Community sought to intervene diplomatically. The Europeans, shocked by the first major violence on the continent in years, scrambled to respond. Aware that the United States wanted to quell the violence, the Europeans took center stage instead. Confident after the fall of the Berlin Wall, and with the Community about to expand into the European Union, one foreign minister, Jacques Poos, hubristically proclaimed the "Hour of Europe" had come. As a result, the European Community deployed negotiators, former British Foreign Secretary Lord Carrington and Portuguese diplomat José Cutileiro, to reach a diplomatic

---

[113] Chuck Sudetic, 'Shelling of Besieged Yugoslav Port Is Intensified', *The New York Times*, 13 November 1991, https://www.nytimes.com/1991/11/13/world/shelling-of-besieged-yugoslav-port-is-intensified.html, [accessed 31 October 2018]

solution.[114]

The conflict in Croatia soon developed an internal Hobbesian logic. Although a federal Yugoslavia still nominally existed, when Slovenia and Croatia declared independence, Belgrade, the JNA, and the Federation basically came to resemble nothing more than a rump state of Serbia. As the JNA moved in to prevent Slovenia and Croatia from leaving the Federation, and also to protect Serbs in Krajina and Slavonia, the mandate appeared to shift. The longer the fighting dragged on, the more it looked as if the JNA was an agent for Serb domination and even conquest.

As Dubrovnik remained under siege, the JNA turned its attention to the Croatian city of Vukovar. With a mixed population of Serbs and Croats, Vukovar lay to the east of Croatia, within the Serb-declared region of Eastern Slavonia. After the declaration of Serb Krajina earlier in 1991, Vukovar became a focal point for tension between Serbs and Croats in the region. Barricades were erected, militias formed, and fighting broke out between groups soon afterwards. The Croat authorities sent forces of under 2,000 to defend the city from a JNA or Serb militia takeover. After the declaration of independence by Zagreb, fighting in and around Vukovar worsened and the JNA did indeed surround the city. From early October 1991, the JNA besieged Vukovar, pummelling it with shells and attempting to starve its inhabitants into submission. The Croat forces defending the city launched offensives against the JNA but were hopelessly outnumbered. JNA troops numbered 36,000, an overwhelming advantage.

The JNA launched their own offensive in November 1991 and took control of the city from the Croats. What followed was chilling, and a harbinger for later events in Bosnia and Herzegovina. In their acclaimed book, *The Death of Yugoslavia*, authors Laura Silber and Allan Little described the aftermath of the Battle of Vukovar as a horrific scene of corpses, chaos and destruction.[115] The Croat population of around 20,000 was forced to leave the city, their homes were looted, and a number of massacres and rapes were carried out by the attacking forces. Many Croats were taken prisoner and detained. Vukovar and its aftermath set the pattern for much of the subsequent fighting, and the city itself would be part of the self-proclaimed Serb Krajina republic until 1995, when Croats retook control of Vukovar.

The negotiators finally brought pressure to bear on the Yugoslavs and the JNA at the end of 1991. A ceasefire was declared in January 1992, and the UN deployed peacekeepers as part of its UN Protection Force (UNPROFOR). The UN "Blue Helmets" were mandated to protect the population in three areas, called "Safe Havens." As a result, the conflict in Croatia was frozen until the summer of 1995.

---

[114] Alan Riding, 'Conflict in Yugoslavia; Europeans send high-level team', *The New York Times*, 29 June 1991, https://www.nytimes.com/1991/06/29/world/conflict-in-yugoslavia-europeans-send-high-level-team.html, [accessed 31 October 2018]

[115] Laura Silber and Allan Little, *The Death of Yugoslavia* (London: Penguin, 1996), p. 180.

The UN and its Security Council had been dormant for much of the Cold War, but now that the superpower confrontation was over, more decisions could be passed without a veto. The early 1990s were a period when the West, now led by a sole superpower, could attempt to mold the international landscape in its image. The UN wanted to enforce international law, self-determination, and human rights standards in Yugoslavia, but there was no consensus on the best approach in the Balkans after 1991. Events in the region threw up devilishly complex challenges where liberal principles contradicted each other. After all, how could national self-determination be applied in ethnically and nationally mixed societies? What was an appropriate use of external force to restore order and prevent further violence? How could minority rights be secured in the successor states? These issues would be hotly debated over the course of the 1990s and only reach some kind of consensus by the time of the Kosovo crisis in 1998-1999.

The Demise of Czechoslovakia

As the Cold War ended in the wake of the fall of the Berlin Wall, the communist countries of Central and Eastern Europe followed a similar pattern. Western advisors and development funds quickly became involved in encouraging these countries to make a transition towards a market economy, and political incentives were also offered so that the countries became liberal democracies that respected human rights and liberal values.

Czechoslovakia was very typical of this era. It moved to a capitalist economy, and while it was more successful than most of its peers, this shift caused some price inflation and unemployment during the transition. It was also offered membership in bodies such as the burgeoning European Union, as well as NATO, if it set up democratic institutions. In November 1990, the Paris Charter was signed, promising a "New Europe" based upon shared democratic and human rights principles. It also laid the framework for a successor to the CSCE by outlining the Organization for Security and Co-operation (OSCE) which would monitor both security and liberal values amongst its members.[116] Czechoslovakia enthusiastically signed up to the Charter.

President Havel was a reluctant politician who had little interest in daily politics and certainly no appetite for detailed economic reform. Nevertheless, he was hugely admired by people in Czechoslovakia and wielded significant moral authority. In 1990, Havel negotiated the final withdrawal of all remaining Soviet military personnel from the country, and he brought in economic advisors who introduced a number of economic reforms and pushed Czechoslovakia in a particularly liberal direction, including broad-ranging privatization. Parliamentary elections were held in June 1990, and Havel's Civic Forum party, led in the parliament by Jan Urban, won 36% of the vote and formed a government with its Slovak counterpart, Public Against Violence. The two parties combined to form a strong majority.

---

[116] OSCE, "Charter of Paris for a New Europe", 21 November 1990, https://www.osce.org/mc/39516, [accessed 7 April 2019]

The months after the end of communism seemed bright for Czechoslovakia, but it would not be long before tensions started to build between Czechs and Slovaks. Havel was a rare figure who could unite different sides and factions, but many other leading politicians of the day, most notably Václav Klaus and Vladimír Mečiar, were prepared to play the national card in their attempts to accrue power.

Klaus

Mečiar

By the early 1990s, it was clear that the Czechs in Czechoslovakia were far wealthier than the Slovaks. Average wealth, measured in 1991, was estimated to be 20% higher for Czechs, and while transfer payments were initially set up from Prague to Bratislava, these ended in 1991. The economic disparity created grievances for Czechs, who resented subsidizing the Slovaks, but it also upset the Slovaks, who felt aggrieved about the Czechs' hold on power. This situation was replicated in many countries during the 1990s, with multinational states proving very fragile. As Cold War spheres of influence diminished, there were no outside forces to rally a multiethnic state around, and there were few restraints if the Czechs and Slovaks wanted to split apart.

The signs began to look ominous for Czechoslovakia in the summer of 1992. Parliamentary elections were held and this time were won by Klaus, an economic liberal and Czech nationalist. Worryingly for federalists such as Havel, Klaus demanded greater centralization, and unless that was achieved, Klaus claimed he would support the fragmentation of Czechoslovakia into two separate states: the Czech Republic and Slovakia.

Leading Slovak politicians, such as Vladimír Mečiar, favored a confederation between the two components, but a growing nationalist sentiment in Slovakia was enough to shift the stance of politicians like Mečiar. On July 17, 1992, the Slovak parliament declared independence.

Incensed, Václav Havel resigned, bitterly opposing dissolution of Czechoslovakia. It was to no avail, however, and that July Klaus and Mečiar agreed to separate Czechoslovakia into two countries. It was not clear that the citizens of either side were particularly enthusiastic about the split, and many still supported the union, but the partition of Czechoslovakia would nonetheless be driven by nationalist politicians on both sides.

To the credit of the politicians who engineered the split of Czechoslovakia into two separate countries, it was quick and peaceful. The other "constructed" states at the end of the First World War and Treaty of Versailles period were not so fortunate. Yugoslavia, for instance, descended into an orgy of violence in the 1990s which shocked Europe and the wider world. There may have been substantial differences in terms of ethnicity, religion, and historic grievances among these multiethnic nations, but regardless, the transition from Czechoslovakia to the independent states of the Czech Republic and Slovakia was remarkably peaceable.

Both separate countries made rapid progress during the 1990s and beyond. The Czech Republic has been one of the success stories of the post-Soviet worl, with one of the lowest unemployment rates in the EU. It has also become home for some of the continent's largest manufacturers, and the Czech Republic is firmly entrenched in the Western system and has a better standard of living than some of the countries that were previously considered to be part of the West, including some in the Mediterranean region.

Both countries were accepted into NATO and then the EU itself in 2004, but the road for Slovakia was somewhat more difficult. Finding prosperity and economic growth to be more of a test, the country's politics have likewise been more challenging. At various times in its quarter of a century of independence, Slovakia has lurched towards populist nationalist politics and even proto-authoritarianism. Vladimír Mečiar became increasingly dictatorial in the 1990s, so much so that the country's upcoming membership in NATO seemed in doubt. As a result, the 1998 parliamentary elections became a referendum on Slovakia's integration into the West. Ultimately, Mečiar's ideas were just about defeated, if not extinguished. Klaus finally stepped down from public life in 2013. Nevertheless, despite consistent support for nationalist, conservative politics, both the Czech Republic and Slovakia are now fixtures of the European Union and secure as NATO members.

The Bosnian War

Much has been written about Western intervention during the breakup of Yugoslavia, and whether it made matters worse, prevented worse atrocities, or was simply ineffective. In early 1992, however, what was clear was that Europe was hopelessly divided over the best course of action to take towards Yugoslavia.

On January 15, 1992, most European countries recognized the independence of Slovenia and Croatia. The matter had caused bitter division between the major European powers. The newly-reunified Germany was the most enthusiastic backer of Slovene and Croat independence, partly for historical reasons and partly due to its huge expatriate community of Croats. France and Britain, however, were opposed, as both countries were traditionally more pro-Serb and were by the early 1990s wary of an expanded Germany throwing its weight around diplomatically.[117] Against European Community protocol, German Foreign Minister Hans Dietrich Genscher unilaterally recognized the two states at the end of 1991, therefore compelling most of the rest of the Community to do likewise a few weeks later.[118] Britain and France were concerned that recognition would set a dangerous precedent and encourage similar actions – and military conflicts – by the competing groups in Bosnia and Herzegovina, as well as alienating the region's largest group, the Serbs.

The role of the United States was more ambiguous.[119] Some accounts of the period have suggested that the US Ambassador in Belgrade, Warren Zimmermann, was strongly in favor of independence for the republics, while others have stated that America had little interest in the Balkan region with so many other foreign challenges taking place, notably the Gulf War and the collapse of the Soviet Union.

On February 29 and March 1 in 1992, Bosnia and Herzegovina held an independence referendum. With a turnout of 63%, almost all respondents voted for independence. Crucially, many Bosnian Serbs boycotted the poll, but shortly afterwards, the country's leader, Alija Izetbegović, declared independence.

---

[117] Vesna Drapac, *Constructing Yugoslavia: A Transnational History*, (Basingstoke: Palgrave Macmillan, 2010), p. 255.

[118] Tom Buchanan, *Europe's Troubled Peace. 1945 to the Present* (Chichester: Wiley-Blackwell, 2012, 2nd ed p. 243.

[119] Alastair Finlan, *The Collapse of Yugoslavia 1991-1999*, (Oxford: Osprey, 2004), p. 44.

Izetbegović

By this point, it was surely clear to the Sarajevo leadership that autonomy would be fraught with difficulty. If Slovenia was a more straightforward proposition than Croatia, then Croatia was less hazardous than Bosnia and Herzegovina. A remnant of the Ottoman Empire, Bosnia had been hailed as recently as the 1984 Sarajevo Winter Olympic Games as a triumph of Yugoslav multiethnic harmony. Wedged in the middle of Yugoslavia, Bosnia and Herzegovina bordered Croatia, Serbia, and Montenegro, and it was divided between Bosniaks (44%), Bosnian Serbs (33%) and Bosnian Croats (17%). The Serbs, who were mainly Orthodox Christians, lived predominantly in the border areas to the east, while the Croats, mainly Catholic, lived in the West. The Bosniaks, who were mainly Muslims, lived in the central parts, including the capital, Sarajevo.

Tensions increased in Bosnia and Herzegovina after Slovenia and Croatia's declarations of independence in June 1991. In some respects, Izetbegović was pushed towards independence hastily and even against his reservations. Nevertheless, it seemed a window had opened, and Bosnia would need to leave Yugoslavia to avoid the tyranny of Milošević.

Bosnian Serbs were also worried that they, like their brethren in Croatia, would be cut adrift from the Federation (and the main Serb Republic) if they were incorporated into a Bosnian state. Preempting a possible move to independence by Sarajevo, the Bosnian Serbs, led by Radovan

Karadžić, called a referendum in November 1991, which resulted in a large majority in favor of staying part of Serbia or Yugoslavia. At the beginning of 1992, Karadžić declared the Bosnian Serb Republic in a similar fashion to Serb Krajina in Croatia.

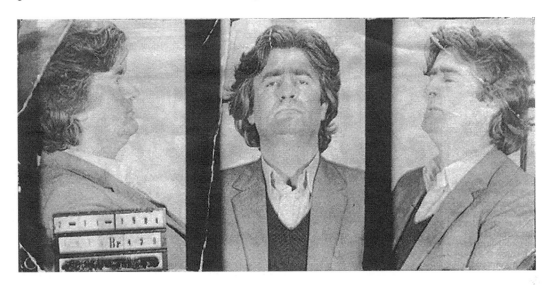

Karadžić

The European negotiators, aware that Bosnia was rapidly becoming a tinderbox, turned their attention to the republic. In March 1992, Carrington and Cutileiro presented a peace plan for Bosnia and Herzegovina, essentially dividing the country into semi-autonomous cantons based on each locality's majority group.[120] The executive and various levels of government and administration would be based upon power-sharing. All three groups accepted the plan on March 18, 1992, with Izetbegović for the Bosniaks, Karadžić for the Serbs, and Mate Boban for the Croats. Izetbegović, however, inexplicably withdrew his support 10 days later following a meeting with Zimmermann in Belgrade. It may be that Izetbegović believed he had been given an assurance of American support for a separate, presumably Bosniak-led version of the state, but regardless, it turned out to be a fateful decision. After the withdrawal, all three groups temporarily retreated, and many of the more hardline factions prepared for the kind of war that had erupted in Croatia the previous year.

The start of hostilities in Bosnia and Herzegovina has been disputed. One account was that the Bosniaks opened fire on a Serb wedding on March 1, while Silber and Little state that the Serb shooting into a crowd of civilians in Sarajevo on April 5 commenced hostilities. What is clear is that after these events, Bosnia and Herzegovina descended into a war more horrific than anything that had occurred since 1945. Apart from the thousands of deaths from fighting between armies and militias, the targeting of civilians was common, especially during the siege of Sarajevo that lasted about three-and-a-half-years. As had been seen in Vukovar in 1991, many people were

---

[120] Josip Glaurdić, *The Hour of Europe: Western Powers and the Breakup of Yugoslavia* (London: Yale University Press, 2011), p. 294.

forced from their homes, held in concentration camps, and even executed on account of their ethnicity. The grim term "ethnic cleansing" moved into the public consciousness during this time.[121]

The politicians had failed to reach a diplomatic agreement in Bosnia and Herzegovina, and one of the great tragedies of the Bosnian example would be that the eventual peace agreement signed in November 1995 would look remarkably similar to the plan rejected in March 1992. Now it was the turn of the military commanders, militia leaders, and a variety of hardliners and extreme nationalists to settle the numerous disputes through force of arms.

Unfortunately for the Bosniaks in particular, it was the JNA which had the majority of the arms, and they were mostly pro-Serb. JNA positions used the hills around Sarajevo to bombard the city daily with artillery fire and cut off supplies. Serb forces made gains around the country throughout 1992 and wasted no time in revealing their malevolent tactics. Serbs took a brutal approach toward civilians in Banja Luka and Srebrenica, and Bosnian President Izetbegović was even taken hostage in May 1992 as he returned to Sarajevo from its airport before being freed after negotiations.[122]

Meanwhile, the international community, especially Britain and France, reinforced the arms embargo to Yugoslavia that had been in place since the previous year. Since the JNA already had a large repository of weapons, the effect of the embargo in practice was to leave the Bosniaks and Bosnian Croats hopelessly exposed to Serb aggression. For its part, UNPROFOR expanded its mission into Bosnia, also setting up safe havens in Srebrenica, Žepa, Goražde, Tuzla and Bihać.

It was soon clear that the violence in Bosnia and Herzegovina would eclipse that in Croatia the previous year. The ferocity of the ethnic killings, the disregard for civilians, the disdain for human rights, the aggression of the propaganda, and the use of concentration camps was wholly different than what had come before it in Yugoslavia's breakup, and once the fighting started in Bosnia, forces were unleashed that were extremely difficult to contain. Whether it was "ancient hatreds" as many commentators believed, wartime memories, or the insecurity and anarchical conditions of the period, the almost immediate brutality on show in Bosnia shocked the world. The early 1990s was a period when 24-hour news channels and satellite television networks came into being, ensuring that the Yugoslav Wars and its grisly footage would be broadcast into people's homes across the world almost daily for four years. After the optimism generated by the end of the Cold War, it was clear that this sense of hope was not shared even throughout Europe. Many observers, journalists, politicians and members of the public decried the inability of governments or the much-vaunted "international community" to do anything about the carnage.

---

[121] Christopher Bennett, *Yugoslavia's Bloody Collapse. Causes, Course and Consequences* (London: Hurst & Company, 1998), p. 238.

[122] Dan Damon, 'When my father was taken captive in Sarajevo', BBC News, 2 May 2012, https://www.bbc.com/news/world-europe-17913518, [accessed 1 November 2018]

That would continue when other atrocities took place during the decade, such as the 1994 Rwandan genocide.

A picture of damage done during the Bosnian War

A picture of damage done during the Siege of Sarajevo

UN Blue Helmets near Sarajevo

The UN increased its role in 1992. In addition to the work of UNPROFOR, the UN authorized a negotiator, former US Secretary of State Cyrus Vance, to work with the newly appointed European negotiator, former British Foreign Secretary David Owen.[123] Both the blue helmets and the negotiators, however, proved ineffective in their objectives. The UN forces were, understandably, supposed to be neutral, and mandated to protect civilians rather than intervene in the fighting. This became a highly difficult task, given that the combatants only had intermittent respect for the neutral position of the UN forces. Occasionally, they even engaged the UN forces.

The negotiators, meanwhile, undertook shuttle diplomacy between Sarajevo and Belgrade, as well as other European capitals and locations in Yugoslavia, in a fruitless attempt to stop the fighting and find a diplomatic solution. They produced a number of peace plans which essentially developed the Carrington-Cutileiro idea further. The Vance-Owen Peace Plan (VOPP) was unveiled in January 1993, proposing the cantons form three separate provinces with Sarajevo having a special status. A successor plan, the Owen-Stoltenberg Plan, produced with Vance's replacement Thorvald Stoltenberg, a Norwegian diplomat, further established these principles.

The problem with the plans was not their formulation, which set out the basis of the eventual peace agreement. Simply put, in 1992 and 1993, the Bosnian Serbs were winning the conflict. With the support of the JNA and Belgrade, and with the arms embargo crippling the Bosniaks, there was no incentive for the Serbs, or Milošević, to compromise. Serb nationalists such as Karadžić could pursue goals of an ethnically homogeneous Greater Serbia, made up of Serbia, the Bosnian Serb areas, Serb Krajina, and Montenegro.

Yugoslav Prime Minister Ante Marković had been forced from an office that essentially no longer existed as Slovenia and Croatia left the Federation. Much later, Marković testified about those final days of Yugoslavia, stating that he was aware of an arrangement made between Slobodan Milošević and Franjo Tudjman in March 1991 at Karađorđevo in Vojvodina to divide up Bosnia and Herzegovina along their own ethnic lines. This alleged agreement has been vigorously denied in the years since, but the Croats would soon enter the fighting.

In 1992, the majority of the fighting in Bosnia took place between the JNA-backed Bosnian Serbs and the rearguard action of the Bosniaks. By the end of the year, Serbs controlled almost 67% of the entire country. As the fighting dragged on into 1993, Bosnian Croats also attacked the Bosniaks. The Sarajevo authorities were now desperately defending their fledgling state from two sides.

Herzegovina was home to many Croats, and in the middle of the ostensibly Bosniak-Serb war, the Croats attempted to set up their own enclave, the "Republic of Herzeg-Bosnia." Similar areas were now dotted across the former Yugoslavia, where the ethnic minority in that country formed an outpost in which its particular group was in the majority, such as Serb Krajina, Slavonia, and

---

[123] David Owen, *Balkan Odyssey* (London: Indigo, 1996)

the Bosnian Serb entity dubbed Republika Srpska (Serb Republic).

Fighting broke out between Bosniaks and Croats, often in a brutal fashion. The Croats made initial gains as the Bosniaks lost more and more territory, impeded as they were by a lack of arms. One visible symbol of this conflict was the destruction of the Stari Most bridge across the Neretva River in the mixed city of Mostar. As fighting escalated, each side took up positions on either side of the bridge until November 9, 1993, when Croat artillery shelled and destroyed the Stari Most. The bridge, an architectural masterpiece, had stood for 427 years.

Josephine W. Baker's picture of the bridge in the 1970s

Eventually, the Bosnian army pushed back Croat forces. Receiving material support from a number of Islamic countries, notably Iran and Pakistan, as well as volunteers, the Bosniaks managed to turn the tide somewhat after their initial setbacks. Partly as a result of this new reality, the Clinton administration pressured the Bosnian Croats to join forces with the Bosniaks in March 1994 as part of the Washington Agreement. The Croat-Bosniak fighting thus ended and the joint Federation of Bosnia and Herzegovina was formed.

Even after they were done fighting each other, Federation forces faced bad odds against the

Serb army. Sarajevo was under constant artillery shelling while snipers around the city would shoot civilians attempting to go about daily life, such as it still existed. A number of particularly horrific bombs destroyed parts of Sarajevo and shocked the outside world, including several marketplace bombs.[124] On August 30, 1992 a Sarajevo marketplace was bombed by a Serb shell, killing 15, and on February 5, 1994, the Markale marketplace was attacked, killing 66.[125]

After each atrocity, international opinion was stirred and hardened against the Serbs. Apart from terrorizing the besieged population, bombing civilians had no strategic purpose and worked as negative propaganda against the Bosnian Serbs, as well as Slobodan Milošević, by now President of Serbia.

The Bosnian War had been raging for three years by the summer of 1995, and UN and European negotiators had tried in vain to bring the various sides to a diplomatic solution. Milošević and Karadžić had proven masters in deception and ambiguity. By that August, the negotiators had all but given up. Whether the Serbs knew the conflict would soon reach a climax is difficult to know, but they embarked upon a course that would finally turn international opinion decisively against them and draw a severe military and diplomatic response from the United States. President Clinton's administration had been infuriated by events in Yugoslavia, and they were disgusted with the leaders on all sides and the UN and European negotiators.

Reports began to emerge about a massacre in the eastern Bosnian town of Srebrenica in July 1995. Home to a large number of Bosnian Muslims, Srebrenica had been delegated a "safe haven" and protected as such by UN blue helmet peacekeepers. The reasons for what happened next is hotly disputed, but Bosnian Serb forces, commanded by General Ratko Mladić, overran the town and peacekeepers, expelling many of the Bosniaks there and leading around 8,000 men and boys into the surrounding countryside to be executed. The Srebrenica massacre was the worst war crime to take place in Europe in 50 years, and it provided ample evidence of a campaign of genocide by the Serbs against the Bosnian Muslims.

---

[124] Bill Clinton, *My Life* (London: Arrow, 2005), p. 581.

[125] John Kifner, '66 Die as Shell Wrecks Sarajevo Market', *The New York Times* 6 February 1994, https://www.nytimes.com/1994/02/06/world/66-die-as-shell-wrecks-sarajevo-market.html, [accessed 1 November 2018]

A picture of massacre victims being exhumed

Mladić

When news of the massacre reached the outside world (Dutch UNPROFOR peacekeepers had been forced to step aside as the victims were taken prisoner), the calls for something to be done reached a fevered pitch. Then, on August 28, 1995, Serb artillery shells hit the Markale marketplace yet again, this time killing 43. This was the final straw for the Clinton administration. A NATO force, Operation Deliberate Force, bombed Bosnian Serb positions in an effort to stop the shelling of civilian areas, including safe havens. The raids led to the deaths of 27 Bosnian Serb soldiers and the same number of Bosnian Serb civilians.

Shortly before the NATO strikes, the Clinton administration approved a secret Croatian offensive to take back the Serb enclaves within its territory. The Croatian armed forces, which had been preparing the operation for some time, were keen to exploit the increased anti-Serb sentiment in the international media, and they overwhelmed the makeshift Serb defences across Krajina. In a matter of days, Croats were in control of their entire territory.

The fates of the Croatian Serbs, however, were grim. Virtually all were forced from their homes and effectively displaced, vilified as a "fifth column" within Croatia. Around 200,000 Croatian Serbs – whose lineage there went back centuries - were displaced and turned into refugees, forced to trudge to the Republika Srpska or Serbia itself. This was another example of ethnic cleansing, albeit a less violent one.

Further NATO airstrikes in late September 1995 put further pressure on the Serbs. By November that year the Serb leadership was on the backfoot after years of obstinence in the face of international condemnation. The leaders of the three main Bosnian nationalities were summoned to the American airbase in Dayton, Ohio in November. Alija Izetbegović, representing the Bosniaks, Franjo Tudjman, representing the Croats, and Slobodan Milošević, representing the Serbs (it was noteworthy that Radovan Karadžić did not travel to Dayton), argued relentlessly, but finally, under pressure and threats from the Clinton administration, they signed a peace treaty.[126]

The Dayton Accords were similar to the previous peace plans set forth by Carrington, Cutileiro, Owen, Vance and Stoltenberg. They ostensibly allowed division in Bosnia and Herzegovina along federal lines, with a Bosniak-Croatian Federation – based at Sarajevo - governing 51% of the country, and a Republika Srpska – based at Banja Luka - controlling the remaining 49%. All levels of government and administration throughout the country would be based upon the principles of power-sharing.

The fighting had ended at the cost of some 250,000 dead and two million people displaced.[127] The wounds of the conflict, however, would take much longer to heal. A better description of the Dayton Accords might have been that they froze the conflict. The Serbs had, more or less, been rewarded for their territorial gains. The Republika Srpska would develop into a nationalistic enterprise whose leadership continues to agitate for independence from the Federation.

---

[126] Bill Clinton, *My Life* (London: Arrow, 2005), pp. 684-685.
[127] Bill Clinton, *My Life* (London: Arrow, 2005), p. 684.

The Bitter End

Yugoslavia was long dead by the time of the Dayton Accords. Bosnia and Herzegovina, Croatia, and Slovenia had all left with varying degrees of difficulty. Macedonia had also declared independence, recognized in 1992, with minimal fuss despite its own mixed population. After Dayton, the name Yugoslavia endured, but now it only included Serbia, Vojvodina, Montenegro and Kosovo.

To the outside world, Milošević – as well as Bosnian Serb leaders such as Ratko Mladic and Radovan Karadžić – appeared most accountable for the carnage of the 1990s in the Balkans. The Serbs may have complained that this was unfair, a simplification of hugely complex forces and events, and indeed, Croatian Serbs had suffered grievously at the end of the conflict. Still, many in the international community concluded that the main culprits in the wars were the Serbs. It didn't help the Serbs that their traditional ally, Russia (which shared Orthodox Christianity with the Serbs), was in crisis and retreat -

Milošević, of course, had drawn a different conclusion. Despite sanctions and international condemnation, Milošević was still in power and essentially presiding over a Greater Serbia, albeit a smaller one than it might've included with sovereignty over Serbian enclaves in Croatia and Bosnia. He personally had not been implicated in any atrocity or war crimes - in fact, he was welcomed in foreign capitals as a peacekeeper, signing peace treaties. It may be that Milošević, who was later deeply implicated in the horrors of the conflicts, felt a sense of impunity. After all, despite the opprobrium directed at the Bosnian Serbs, a policy of territorial conquest and ethnic cleansing had at least partially paid dividends.

It was against this backdrop that the final major act in the history of Yugoslavia played out in Kosovo.

Croat nationalists had sought independence for much of the Federation's existence. Bosnia and Herzegovina had much less of a tradition of separatism, but both were excruciatingly divided from Yugoslavia due to large Serb minorities who opposed separation or wanted their own separate status. Kosovo, however, was a different topic altogether. The province was considered an integral part of Serbia, crucial to understanding the Serb nation and its defining moment of awakening on the battlefield in 1389. Slobodan Milošević had exploited this strong nationalist attachment during his speech there on the occasion of the battle's 600th anniversary in June 1989.

The reality of life in 20th century Kosovo, however, was somewhat detached from these romantic notions. Kosovo was 90% ethnic Albanian, with only a tiny minority of Serbs. Tensions had increased after Tito's death in 1980, and Kosovar Albanians had demonstrated in 1981, seeking greater cultural recognition. On the other side, Serbs had protested in 1987 over alleged discrimination and police prejudice.[128] The latter episode had led to Milošević's trip there and his subsequent positioning as defender of the Serbs. Milošević had subsequently installed his own supporters in positions of authority in Kosovo, apparently dampening the disturbances.

In the late 1980s and much of the 1990s, Kosovo was experiencing a cold peace, but Kosovar Albanians dreamed of their own imperial project, Greater Albania, which would include Albania, Kosovo, and parts of Macedonia. They perceived that their moment might be approaching after the four republics had left Yugoslavia and life under Milošević's rule would surely not be pleasant for Albanians in Kosovo, particularly after the Serb strongman had forged his reputation on the ethnic issue.

In 1991, the Kosovo Liberation Army (KLA) was formed. Styled more on an outdated Cold War model of national independence through armed tactics, mainly of the guerrilla variety, the KLA presented a different challenge than the political movements of Slovenia, Croatia, and Bosnia and Herzegovina. The KLA began to target Serb police and government installations, as well as civilians, in 1995.[129] Throughout this time, weapons and equipment were smuggled to the guerrillas via Albania.

Certainly, the ethnic Albanian population had suffered oppression, especially after Milošević had come to power, but at a different time, the KLA would probably have been portrayed as an illegal, violent group which the government was attempting to defeat. The previous carnage in the region changed all that, and with the Serbs being blamed for the violence, the KLA was viewed somewhat sympathetically. Moreover, Western politicians were anxious to prevent a replay of those conflicts in Kosovo.

A campaign of sabotage increased in 1997, while ethnic tensions simmered between Kosovar Serbs and Albanians. The pattern worsened that year as a result of events in neighboring Albania. The loss of authority in March 1997 of Albanian President Berisha led to military repositories and arsenals being looted, meaning the country was suddenly awash with weapons. As anarchy descended on Albania, many of these weapons found their way into the hands of the KLA. Then, in a pattern reminiscent of the conflicts in Croatia and Bosnia, as the minority Serbs became fearful of the majority, many took matters into their hands.

Naturally, Milošević promised to defend the Serb population at any cost. In March 1998, the Yugoslav army again intervened, attacking KLA positions. The violence escalated over the next year, and a familiar pattern of ethnic cleansing, looting, and displacement all played out. Everything was covered once more by the international media, and when scenes of refugees and ethnic Albanians desperately fleeing Serb aggression reached a global audience, the West decided to act.

---

[128] Laura Silber and Allan Little, *The Death of Yugoslavia* (London: Penguin, 1995)

[129] Peter Beaumont, 'KLA goes on killing rampage', *The Guardian*, 27 June 1999, https://www.theguardian.com/world/1999/jun/27/balkans2, [accessed 1 November 2018]

Western politicians were desperate not to watch a repeat of the fighting in Bosnia, and the Clinton administration had been scarred by events involving American forces in Somalia. Throughout the rest of his time in office, military action consisted almost solely of airstrikes. The high-tech US Air Force force was praised for its precision bombing ability, and importantly for Clinton, this approach avoided American casualties.

A NATO summit was held in the French castle of Rambouillet in January 1999, and Milošević was put on notice that if he did not end the campaign of ethnic cleansing, NATO would be forced to intervene. Not satisfied with the response but unable to secure a UN Security Council Resolution on the matter (by 1999, Russia had regained enough composure to offer Serbia its support), NATO launched an air campaign in March 1999. The air strikes lasted for several months, without the desired effect of forcing a withdrawal. In fact, on May 7, NATO bombs hit the Chinese embassy in Belgrade, killing three and causing an international incident.[130]

British Prime Minister Tony Blair, who had then been in office for less than two years, took a keen interest in the conflict. The previous wars had convinced Blair that the West had a moral duty to intervene when it could to prevent human rights abuses. Blair would pursue his principle of humanitarian intervention in Kosovo. The key to success, Blair believed, was to pose the threat of an American-led ground invasion. Once that was credibly on the table, then Milošević would back down.

Clinton and Tony Blair were close allies but very nearly fell out over this matter. Clinton was opposed to the use of American soldiers to back up any threat. In the end, however, Blair convinced the American president, and once a ground invasion was set in motion. In response, the army was indeed quickly withdrawn by Milošević, and the Kosovo War was over by the middle of June 1999.

The outcome was similar to what took place in Bosnia and Herzegovina. A UN Protectorate was established in Kosovo, which lasted until 2008, when the Kosovar authorities declared independence, much to the outrage of Belgrade. For all intents and purposes, the conflict in Kosovo, like Bosnia, is still frozen. Tony Blair would go on to consider the Kosovo intervention a defining success, and it would guide his policies, most notably his support for the 2003 Iraq invasion.

Kosovo was the final straw for Yugoslavia's viability. The violence that had gripped Kosovo spilled over the border with Macedonia, where a latent conflict almost took hold between Macedonians and ethnic Albanians. This time, however, international negotiators entered the fray effectively. Under the auspices of NATO, the "Ohrid Agreement" was signed in August 2001 as a means of adapting the Macedonian constitution to ensure Albanian rights.

---

[130] Steven Lee Meyers, 'Chinese Embassy Bombing: A Wide Net of Blame', *The New York Times*, 17 April 2000, https://www.nytimes.com/2000/04/17/world/chinese-embassy-bombing-a-wide-net-of-blame.html, [accessed 1 November 2018]

By this time, Milošević had finally been removed from office. After the 1999 Kosovo War, he was indicted by the International Criminal Tribunal for the former Yugoslavia in the Hague for war crimes there, as well as in Bosnia and Croatia. Milošević refused to surrender himself and stood for reelection in 2000. When it appeared that the results had been fixed by Milošević, crowds took to the streets of Belgrade demanding he step down, which he finally did on October 6, 2000. A few months later, Yugoslav authorities handed Milošević over to the Hague tribunal. Although he stood trial, Milošević never received a sentence due to dying in prison of a heart attack in 2006. His former mentor and rival, Ivan Stambolić, was assassinated in 2000. After an inquest by the authorities, Milošević was found to have arranged a mafia-style "hit."[131]

Yugoslavia formally folded in 2006 after Montenegrins voted in a referendum to leave the Federation, though in reality, Yugoslavia had not truly existed for several years. Today, the states of the former Yugoslavia are either EU members or candidates. The latter face huge challenges to fulfill this ambition. Apart from the often authoritarian and corrupt political systems in place, these states need to resolve outstanding territorial claims before they can achieve membership. Needless to say, the hangover caused by the disintegration of Yugoslavia has turned out to be long and painful.

The demise of Yugoslavia disconcerted Western society and led to much soul-searching after the fact. Many wondered how a country that seemed financially successful for long stretches could come apart at the seams so quickly and spectacularly. But as any examination of the complete history of the state demonstrates, it faced significant challenges from its very inception. Perhaps the story of Yugoslavia should focus more on how the multinational state survived as long as it did.

Online Resources

Other books about 20th century history by Charles River Editors

Other books about Yugoslavia on Amazon

Other books about Czechoslovakia on Amazon

Further Reading about Yugoslavia

Badredine Arfi, *International Change and the Stability of Multiethnic States. Yugoslavia, Lebanon, and Crises of Governance.* (Indianapolis: Indiana University Press, 2005)

David Binder, 'A Coffin for Mihailovic', *New York Times*, 10 February 1991, https://www.nytimes.com/1991/02/10/books/a-coffin-for-mihailovic.html

---

[131] Vesna Peric Zimonjic, 'Death squad leader guilty of killing Serbian president', *The Independent,* 19 July 2005, https://www.independent.co.uk/news/world/europe/death-squad-leader-guilty-of-killing-serbian-president-300063.html, [accessed 1 November 2018]

Nada Boskovska, *Yugoslavia and Macedonia Before Tito: Between Repression and Integration* (London: IB Tauris, 2016)

Christopher Catherwood, *Churchill and Tito: SOE, Bletchley Park and Supporting the Yugoslav Communists in World War II* (Frontline Books, 2017)

Dejan Djokić, 'Versailles and Yugoslavia: ninety years on', *Open Democracy*, 26 June 2009, https://www.opendemocracy.net/article/versailles-and-yugoslavia-ninety-years-on

Dejan Djokić, *Pasic & Trumbic: The Kingdom of Serbs, Croats and Slovenes.* (Haus Publishing, 2010)

Vesna Drapac, *Constructing Yugoslavia: A Transnational History*, (Basingstoke: Palgrave Macmillan, 2010)

Richard J. Evans, *The Pursuit of Power: Europe 1815-1914* (London: Penguin, 2017)

Tom Gallagher, *Outcast Europe: The Balkans, 1789-1989: From the Ottomans to Milošević*, (London: Routledge, 2001)

Robert Gerwarth, *The Vanquished: Why the First World War Failed to End, 1917-1923* (London: Allen Lane, 2016)

Ivo Goldstein, 'The Independent State of Croatia in 1941: On the Road to Catastrophe', *Totalitarian Movements and Political Religions*, 7:4, 2006, pp. 417-427

Misha Glenny, *The Balkans 1804-2012: Nationalism, War and the Great Powers* (London: Granta, 2012)

The History Channel, '1941: Yugoslavia joins the Axis', (A&E Networks, 2009), https://www.history.com/this-day-in-history/yugoslavia-joins-the-axis

Godfrey Hodgson, *People's Century: From the dawn of the century to the eve of the millennium* (Godalming: BBC Books, 1998)

Paul Kennedy, *The Rise and Fall of the Great Powers: Economic Change and Military Conflict from 1500 to 2000* (New York: Random House, 1987)

James M. Lindsay, 'TWE Remembers: Austria-Hungary Issues an Ultimatum to Serbia', *Council on Foreign Relations*, 23 July 2014, https://www.cfr.org/blog/twe-remembers-austria-hungary-issues-ultimatum-serbia

Sonia Lucarelli, *Europe and the Breakup of Yugoslavia. A Political Failure in Search of a Scholarly Explanation*, (The Hague: Kluwer Law International, 2000)

Oto Luthar (ed), *The Land Between: A History of Slovenia* (Frankfurt am Main: Peter Lang, 2008)

Blanka Matkovich, *Croatia and Slovenia at the End and After the Second World War (1944-1945): Mass Crimes and Human Rights Violations Committed by the Communist Regime*, (Brown Walker Press, 2017)

Mark Mazower, *The Balkans: From the End of Byzantium to the Present Day* (London: Phoenix, 2001)

Eugene Michail, 'Western Attitudes to War in the Balkans and the Shifting Meanings of Violence, 1912-1991', *Journal of Contemporary History*, (47:219, 2012), 219-241.

Eugene Michail, *The British and the Balkans. Forming Images of Foreign Lands, 1900-1950.* (London: Continuum, 2011)

David Owen, *Balkan Odyssey* (London: Indigo, 1996)

Laura Silber and Allan Little, *The Death of Yugoslavia* (London: Penguin, 1996)

Brendan Simms, *Europe: The Struggle for Supremacy 1453 to the Present* (London: Penguin, 2014)

Brendan Simms, *Unfinest Hour: Britain and the Destruction of Bosnia*, (London: Penguin, 2001)

Further Reading about Czechoslovakia

BBC News, "1989: Police crush Prague protest rally", http://news.bbc.co.uk/onthisday/hi/dates/stories/november/17/newsid_2540000/2540171.stm

Christopher Clark, *The Sleepwalkers: How Europe Went to War in 1914* (London: Penguin, 2013)

Francis Fukuyama, "The End of History?" *The National Interest*, 16 (1989), pp. 3-18.

Mary Fulbrook, *History of Germany, 1918-2000: the divided nation* (Oxford: Blackwell, 2002)

Misha Glenny, *The Balkans 1804-2012: Nationalism, War and the Great Powers* (London: Granta, 2012)

Jussi M. Hanhimaki, *The Rise and Fall of Détente. American Foreign Policy and the Transformation of the Cold War* (Washington DC: Potomac Books)

Godfrey Hodgson, *People's Century: From the dawn of the century to the eve of the millennium* (Godalming: BBC Books, 1998)

Robert Hutchings, 'American Diplomacy and the End of the Cold War in Europe', *Foreign Policy Breakthroughs: Cases in Successful Diplomacy*, ed. Robert Hutchings and Jeremi Suri (Oxford: Oxford University Press, 2015, pp. 148-172)

Gerald Knaus, "Europe and Azerbaijan: The End of Shame", *Journal of Democracy,* (2015, pp. 5-18)

W. Mayr, 'Hungary's Peaceful Revolution Cutting the Fence and Changing History', *Der Spiegel*, 29 May 2009, http://www.spiegel.de/international/europe/hungary-s-peaceful-revolution-cutting-the-fence-and-changing-history-a-627632.html

Norman M. Naimark, *The Russians in Germany: A History of the Soviet Zone of Occupation, 1945-1949* (Harvard: Harvard University Press, 1995)

The New York Times, "Police Attack Protesters at Prague Demonstration", 29 October 1988, https://www.nytimes.com/1988/10/29/world/police-attack-protesters-at-prague-demonstration.html, [accessed 2 April 2019]

The New York Times, "The Gorbachev Visit; Excerpts From Speech to U.N. on Major Soviet Military Cuts", 8 December 1988, https://www.nytimes.com/1988/12/08/world/the-gorbachev-visit-excerpts-from-speech-to-un-on-major-soviet-military-cuts.html [accessed 2 April 2019]

OSCE, "Charter of Paris for a New Europe", 21 November 1990, https://www.osce.org/mc/39516

Jiri Pehe, "The Other Vaclav: How the Czech president became Europe's public enemy number one", *The New York Times*, 12 October 2009

Prague Morning, "81 Years Ago Today, Tomas G. Masaryk Died", http://www.praguemorning.cz/81-years-ago-today-tomas-g-masaryk-died-kclvjTJiBd

Ferdinand Protzman, 'Jubilant East Germans Cross to West in Sealed Trains', *New York Times*, 6 October 1989, http://www.nytimes.com/1989/10/06/world/jubilant-east-germans-cross-to-west-in-sealed-trains.html

Reuters, "Czechs mark 50 years since Jan Palach's self-immolation over crushing of Prague Spring", 16 January 2019, https://www.reuters.com/article/us-czech-anniversary-palach/czechs-mark-50-years-since-jan-palachs-self-immolation-over-crushing-of-prague-spring-idUSKCN1PA2BO

Marci Shore, "Review: 'Havel: A Life,' by Michael Zantovsky", *The New York Times*, 26 December 2014, https://www.nytimes.com/2014/12/28/books/review/havel-a-life-by-michael-zantovsky.html

John Tagliabue, Prague Jails a Major Playwright For Inciting Protests Last Month, *The New York Times*, 22 February 1989, https://www.nytimes.com/1989/02/22/world/prague-jails-a-major-playwright-for-inciting-protests-last-month.html

John Tagliabue, Czech Playwright Released From Prison, *The New York Times*, 18 May 1989, https://www.nytimes.com/1989/05/18/world/czech-playwright-freed-from-prison.html

Emily Tamkin, "In Charter 77, Czech Dissidents Charted New Territory", *Foreign Policy*, 3 February 2017, https://foreignpolicy.com/2017/02/03/in-charter-77-czech-dissidents-charted-new-territory/

Ed Vulliamy, "Terezín: 'The music connected us to the lives we had lost'", *The Guardian*, 5 April 2013, https://www.theguardian.com/music/2013/apr/05/terezin-nazi-camp-music-eva-clarke

Free Books by Charles River Editors

We have brand new titles available for free most days of the week. To see which of our titles are currently free, click on this link.

Discounted Books by Charles River Editors

We have titles at a discount price of just 99 cents everyday. To see which of our titles are currently 99 cents, click on this link.

Made in the USA
Las Vegas, NV
03 August 2021